GERALDINE A. LARKIN

WOMAN TO WOMAN

STREET SMARTS FOR WOMEN ENTREPRENEURS

PRENTICE HALL
Englewood Cliffs, New Jersey 07632

Prentice-Hall International (UK) Limited, *London*
Prentice-Hall of Australia Pty. Limited, *Sydney*
Prentice-Hall Canada, Inc., *Toronto*
Prentice-Hall Hispanoamericana, S.A., *Mexico*
Prentice-Hall of India Private Limited, *New Delhi*
Prentice-Hall of Japan, Inc., *Tokyo*
Simon & Schuster Asia Pte. Ltd., *Singapore*
Editora Prentice-Hall do Brasil, Ltda., *Rio de Janeiro*

10 9 8 7 6 5 4 3 2 1

Library of Congress Cataloging-in-Publication Data

Larkin, Geraldine A.
  Woman to woman: street smarts for women entrepreneurs /
Geraldine A. Larkin.
      p.   cm.
  Includes bibliographical references and index.
  ISBN 0-13-706658-9
  1. Women in business—United States. 2. Women-owned busi-
ness enterprises—United States. 3. Entrepreneurship—United
States. I. Title.
  HD6054.4.U6L37   1993   93-4260
  658.4′21′082—dc20   CIP

ISBN 0-13-706658-9

PRENTICE HALL
Career & Personal Development
Englewood Cliffs, NJ 07632

Simon & Schuster, A Paramount Communications Company

Printed in the United States of America

KENNEDY

About the Author

As the 1992 Business Advocate of the Year for Michigan's women entrepreneurs Dr. Geri Larkin has spent most of her adult life in the trenches helping women to build their businesses.

With an undergraduate degree from Barnard College in New York City and a Ph.D. from Portland State University in Oregon, Dr. Larkin first spent five years at the C. S. Mott Foundation funding nonprofits in the area of economic development. From there she worked with technology-based companies to raise financing. Since 1988 Geri has been with the international management consulting firm of Deloitte & Touche. As the Senior Manager for Emerging Businesses for its Michigan Practice she spends her days midwiving businesses from conception through "their [chaotic] teenage" years.

Dr. Larkin holds positions on numerous boards, ranging from the Michigan Technology Council to her church.

Introduction

So it begins, this journey of yours. With *Woman to Woman* I have tried my best to walk you through all of the steps you'll take starting and building a successful business. Beginning with background, Chapter 1 reviews the characteristics of successful entrepreneurs—what it takes to run a business. The surprise is that most of us have what it takes. I simply emphasized the parts of your persona that you will be working the hardest. It also takes a look at both the upside and downside of owning a business so you can move forward with your eyes open. And I talk about teams because, yes, you'll be building one even if you simply want to be self-employed.

Chapter 2 continues the background discussion by talking you through your own likes and dislikes, starting from childhood. I do this because I've learned that women who develop businesses based on what they love really are successful and that the pattern of what they love starts from childhood. Chapter 2 also discusses different types of business options. You could purchase a franchise or buy an existing business—there are many ways to get started. Or you can simply start from scratch.

You'll see I become more opinionated as I go. Chapter 3 is fierce. In it I am determined to convince you to stay away from partnerships. You'll also find a list of the types of legal documents you need as well as a listing of the advantages and disadvantages of different business structures. I beg you to buy a computer and forgo plants and new furniture.

Money issues are covered in Chapters 4 and 5. Starting with all the reasons why you need a good credit history, Chapter 4 walks you through budgets, bookkeeping systems and cash flow. Perhaps more than any other knowledge, you need to "get" cash flow so you can use financial records as a management tool. Chapter 5 is about finding money. Most women wait too long. Or assume they'll never need to raise money for their business. Well, one out of a hundred of you is right. But 99 are wrong. Virtually all of us need to raise financing at some point in growing a business. It can be equity, debt, royalty financing, a combination of these, or something creative. Chapter 5 teaches you how to think about financing and prepares you for the types of questions investors will ask.

Much of what they will want to know can be summarized in your business plan. As a long-term writer of business plans, I don't know how you can run a business without one. It's a road map, a life line, a teddy bear—it's your comfort blanket. Chapter 6 talks you through its parts.

Finding the right people to manage is one of the most difficult and time-consuming tasks of any business owner. My biases surface again in Chapter 7 when I urge you not to hire the people closest to you and then walk you through the steps of hiring wisely. I also review clues which will tell you when it is time to start looking and even added a chart you can actually use yourself as you hire staff. Negotiation skills are covered because you'll need them more than ever. And finally, Chapter 7 covers firing—all business owners' least favorite chore.

The last third of *Woman to Woman* aims at your life on a more personal level. Because time is critical, setting priorities is covered, as is learning to say no and why business lunches are a lousy idea. You'll learn why delegation is crucial to your success and how to do it well.

Chapter 9 applauds your intuitive skills as we walk through the process of understanding your market and where you fit. It also reviews the importance of public relations and how to keep them on your priority list.

Success means selling. If no one buys your product, you won't be in business for very long. Since selling is terrifying to most rational people, you'll find a detailed description of how to sell by listening well—and by asking for the sale in Chapter 10.

By Chapter 11 you'll be ready to hear about retirement—so it's covered there. Retiring always starts with understanding your finances as well as knowing what the Internal Revenue Service expects of you as an owner of a business. Since tracking expenses is a key to staying on the IRS' good side, you'll find expense charts in that chapter. Tax investing is also covered, as are estate planning, the importance of writing a will—and life insurance.

And finally, you need to take care of yourself. Chapters 12 and 13 offer guidelines for doing just that. My last bout of begging has to do with trying to convince you of the importance of balance in your life (not that I'm that good at it myself) and why you need to take time off. Exercise is covered—so is what you eat. I talk about how emotionally vulnerable women can be when they build their businesses and give you a checklist to help you watch for potential problems with relationships—particularly emerging ones. I also cover ethics—because they matter.

Chapter 13 completes *Woman to Woman* with a checklist of where you can get help. Sources are as varied as your accountant, mentors, associations, database search services and people you can trust.

I figured thirteen chapters was plenty. Maybe even too much for one sitting—but I decided to write everything I knew anyway.

Just remember: I'm pulling for you every minute of every day.

From start to finish *Woman to Woman: Street Smarts for Women Entrepreneurs* has as its goal talking readers through the real rules of starting and building a business. Based on real life experience, the book starts with the premise that you need to build on what you love to do and goes from there. Then, step by step, virtually all aspects of building a business are covered—from what its structure should be to writing a business plan—from marketing to sales to where to get honest advice. *Woman to Woman* is specific. It gives readers checklists for hiring and firing, for how to choose the type of business to start or buy, for a marketing campaign, and more.

The book will be one of the "musts" for every woman business owner's library—a comfort station, a friend, a source of solutions to the problems faced by all female entrepreneurs.

<u>SUBJECTS</u>	<u>WHY OF INTEREST</u>
1. What type of business should you start?	Most women have a tough time deciding what type of business to go into.
2. Legal issues.	This is scary stuff—but women want to know.
3. The role family, friends and mates play	These are issues most women in a business want to know about, few people talk about and no one tells them the truth until they find out for themselves the hard way.
4. The business plan.	This chapter is as user-friendly as it gets—most entrepreneurs know they need to write a business plan, they just don't know how to get started.
5. Money—understanding cash flow.	User-friendly.

6. Finding financing

This is just like the mating dance. Readers get a step-by-step process of how to think about and then look for financing.

7. Keeping your sanity.

Another taboo subject no one talks about. The book emphasizes the need for balance, boundaries and surrounding oneself with truly trustworthy people.

THANK YOU

To all the male bosses and associates who have taught me their rules, most recently Michael Cleland and Sandy Duncan, partners with Deloitte & Touche.

To all the women business owners I've laughed with, cried with, and worked with to find financing, to write business plans, and to become the leaders they were meant to be.

To my whole family, especially my mother. She taught me to *look*. Also, Jamie, who puts in a lot of time without her mommy.

To Tom Power, my editor. He believed me first.

Preface

I've made all the mistakes. I've told a banker that he should give me a loan because I needed it instead of talking about what a low risk I was to the bank. I've hired the wrong people. I've fired the wrong people. I've tried to work with a mate—several times, in fact, because I can be a slow learner when it suits me. I've even considered hiring my mother. As I look back at my behavior and that of the hundreds of women I've worked with over the years, I've noticed that my "mistakes" were of two types. The first simply had to do with being new at running a business. The second had to do with being a woman. I've come to believe, as a male friend keeps telling me, that women and men really are from different planets. At least ours is Venus. Women bring a different world view to the business table that, in our formative years as business owners, can hurt us. This is changing. The new models are out there. Some of the best are described in a wonderful book by Joline Godfrey, *Our Wildest Dreams*. But, the fact is that the business world is still male-led, with male rules. And it will be for a while yet. And when a woman doesn't know the rules and when her femaleness doesn't match the male environment, she is at a terrible disadvantage. In my view. After more than twelve years of watching.

I don't think you need to make the mistakes I've made. Or the other women who have come before you. The street smarts are out there—we've learned them. It's just that no one has taken the time to share them out loud. Until now. That is my gift to you.

CONTENTS

HOW TO TELL
IF YOU HAVE
THE RIGHT STUFF

Your expectations are what come true. Brian Tracey

THE STATISTICS

The numbers tell the story. In 1960, 3 percent of all businesses were owned by women. In 1970, it was 5 percent; in 1980, 26 percent. The National Foundation for Women Business Owners in Washington, D.C., tells us that more than 5.4 million women now own businesses in this country. At this rate of growth, we'll own more than half of all businesses by the year 2000. Grin. We employ more people than all of the Fortune 500 companies combined—11.7 million people. And while jobs at the top corporations declined at a rate of 200,000 to 300,000 in 1992 alone, women-owned businesses added 350,000 employees. Our businesses are growing at five times the rate of other small firms—making us the fastest growing business segment in the country.

And we don't fail. While close to 40 percent of all male-owned businesses fail, for women the number is closer to 20 percent.

We're a tidal wave. One that has the potential of changing the entire structure of U.S. business—bringing care and concern and love and fun to the plate—finally.

WHO ARE THESE WOMEN?

Who is out there already? Who are the women who have already taken the risk to start their own firms and have lived to tell about it? What are their characteristics and, most critical to you, are you made of the same right stuff?

In *Our Wildest Dreams*, Joline Godfrey describes the women business owners she has met as "ordinary" in this sense: they are your sisters, your friends, your daughters, your partners—they are you and me.

And she's right. The hundreds of women business owners that I know all have the same concerns you and I have. They have kids, some have spouses, they cook the meals, most still clean their houses. None has a wife (well, okay, one does). Very few are children of wealth. They were all scared out of their wits when they started. Most didn't sleep well for months. Some still don't.

And there is something else. These women have the courage to take a risk. They aren't afraid to try things. They want to be *who they are* and not how anyone else wants them to be and that is one heck of a motivating force. To a woman, they are good at relationships. They want to connect with other people. They feel intensely, they think intensely and they are right where they are in the moment. (No daydreaming for these women!) Most were comfortable in a business environment before they started the company. Above all, they are survivors. Sometimes they laugh until they're sick when they think of all the mistakes they've all made on the way—yet each woman has survived and grown and is in some way better for the lesson learned. And she wouldn't go back.

THE ATTRIBUTES OF SUCCESS

In 1989, Avon Products did a survey of entrepreneurs to discover what makes women entrepreneurs successful and found some surprising information. First off, they discovered that only 9 percent of successful women started their business to make a lot of money (or even more money for that matter). Instead, over and over women said they simply wanted more control over their lives. Other reasons for starting ranged from someone else talking them into it (although this is quite rare) to an opportunity falling into a woman's lap. Success was not measured in money, but in how happy and fulfilled the business owner felt. About 30 percent of the women saw success as the achievement of simply opening a business—any business. Another 20 percent said they measured their success by their ability to help other people.

What worked? Surprisingly, business experience was not the major predictor of business success. So if you've been postponing your start-up until you complete your MBA, you can stop waiting. In my experience, MBAs help only when people have been taught by professors with entrepreneurial backgrounds.

What was it about the women themselves that made it work? Two things. Perseverance was the first. The women surveyed refused to give up their vision. They simply refused. I see this over and over and over. In the olden days (before I had any idea what I was doing) when people asked me to predict whether someone's business would succeed, I used to rattle off skills like management and marketing. Over time, I've seen that while those skill sets matter, the real measure of whether a woman will make it or not has to do with her sheer determination to make it work. Any woman who has decided to lose fifteen pounds in a month knows exactly what I mean. You just keep at it until you get it. Perseverance.

The second indicator of success in the Avon study had to do with attitude. Optimists succeed. Pessimists don't. Optimists believe that there is a way out of every corner—and you'll find yourself in lots of corners. Pessimists don't.

Other things that you might expect to matter, didn't. Education level doesn't matter. Neither does marital status, although it seems to me I slept better in former days when, as a married woman, I knew there was another income coming in. Whether or not you have children seems to be a nonissue. So is race, in that being a woman in what is still a male world is challenging for all females.

YOUR OWN PREDICTOR TEST

How can you tell if you're a "right stuff" woman? If I were sitting with you now I would tell you that you already are, but I've learned through time that women have to discover this truth for themselves. Let me just say that seven out of ten women will do something entrepreneurial in their lifetime. If you think about it, you'll know which 3 friends out of ten you can picture who won't be starting a business—so that leaves you in, right? Or you wouldn't be reading this book in the first place.

If you still need proof, you can fill out the following checklist.

1. Can you work long hours with little sleep? ❑ YES ❑ NO
2. Can you tolerate uncertainty? ❑ YES ❑ NO
3. Do you take risks? ❑ YES ❑ NO
4. Do you enjoy taking risks? ❑ YES ❑ NO
5. Do you have high self-confidence? ❑ YES ❑ NO
6. Are you persistent? ❑ YES ❑ NO
7. Do you know how to set goals and objectives for yourself? ❑ YES ❑ NO

8. Can you meet those goals and objectives? ❏ YES ❏ NO

9. Do you enjoy facing obstacles to see what it will take to get past them? ❏ YES ❏ NO

10. Do you know how to use failure as a learning experience? ❏ YES ❏ NO

11. Do you ask for help and advice when you need it? ❏ YES ❏ NO

12. Can you accept responsibility for important decisions? ❏ YES ❏ NO

13. Do you have the ability to become totally immersed in the building of a business? ❏ YES ❏ NO

14. Are you always ethical? ❏ YES ❏ NO

15. Do you like to "take charge"? ❏ YES ❏ NO

16. Are you always reliable? ❏ YES ❏ NO

17. Do you always deal honestly with other people? ❏ YES ❏ NO

If you checked more "yes" choices, you are well on your way to building a business.

If you did not check "yes" to everything, your goal should be to develop yourself to where you can answer each question affirmatively.

WHAT THE CHECKLIST MEANS

Let me discuss each one and why it is important:

1. Long hours and little sleep. The average entrepreneur works around sixty hours a week. In a recent survey by American Express, 80 percent of business owners said they worked between sixty and sixty-nine hours a week. In the first year, this can go up to eighty hours or more. Since most women still have the obligations of keeping up a home, cooking, and possibly child rearing, not to mention mating obligations, those hours can be hard to find. Most women simply sleep less. So, if you don't know how to function on six hours of sleep a night, it might be time to practice. Less than that can be dangerous. I know most women reading this will smile, knowing they've been going on six hours of sleep for all their adult lives—I just wanted to confirm that you won't have any more to look forward to for a while.

2. *Tolerating uncertainty.* Wise women tell us that nothing is certain in life. While that may be true, I for one like it when some things at least appear to be certain in my life. When you own a business, however, *nothing* is certain. You never know for sure if you will have customers. You never know where they'll come from. You're never quite sure what they'll buy. You never know if they'll pay. Or when they'll pay. Or how they'll pay. You never know if your staff will stay or where you'll find your staff in the first place. You don't know where competition will come from or what your current competition is going to do next. If you need certainty in your life, owning a business may not be for you.

3. *Risk taking.* Taking risks means making decisions and taking actions without knowing the result. This is courage. Charlotte Taylor, a longtime wise woman in this field, once shared with me the intrinsic components of risk taking listed below. To be a risk taker, you need to be willing to:

- Simply let go.
- Pay the price of the decision or action.
- Change if you need to.
- Look foolish occasionally.
- Go against people you love.

- Be rejected by people for whom you care.
- Be uncomfortable because something is always new.
- Lose "face."
- Lose everything you've ever worked for.

Women with the "right stuff" take risks every day. On the color of the brochure. When they locate in a particular place. Whenever they develop a product. When they sell. Hire. Choose a bank. Every day. The best risk takers simply make the decision, or do the action, and just keep moving forward without obsessing too much about the consequences of the decision. As Marlo Thomas puts it, "When we line up all the facts that we believe are against us, the facts can stop us before we start. Whatever we need to discourage us—'I'm too young, too old, too short, too tall, unprepared, inexperienced or not quite ready'—we can uncover. And if we miss a few details, we can always find someone to help us 'face the facts.' The facts, after all, speak for themselves—except they're not true. Courage is doing it anyway, whatever *it* is. We all doubt ourselves . . . we all wonder whether we really have the goods."

Which brings me to the next point. Taking risks can be great fun. Sort of like playing Monopoly. Women who enjoy taking risks are not afraid to make decisions when they need to. And they are excited about experiencing the consequences of the decision.

4. High self-confidence. Women business owners who succeed have high self-confidence. They believe deeply in themselves and in their ability to figure out what needs to be done in a specific situation. In the American Express Travel Related Services Company survey mentioned earlier, 82 percent of all successful entrepreneurs put their chance of survival at 9 out of 10 or better at the outset. That is self-confidence.

5. Persistence. Webster's New World Dictionary (1986) defines persistence as a stubbornness, an ability to endure continuance and tenacity. There is a stubborn quality to most of the women I work with. They are determined that their business will succeed. There is no half-heartedness about it. It is also clear that these women are in it for the long haul—as in years. You won't even know what the real potential of your business is for the first year and a half. At that point, most of you will be just beginning to experience your first sales. Persistence is your willingness to stay in the game *for as long as it takes.*

6. Goals and objectives. More on this later. Let me just say that it takes an ability to set (and meet) goals and objectives to succeed in business. What are they? Tangible measures of what you are trying to do with your company. Your goal is simply what you are trying to attain as a company. For example, a goal might be to be the best day-care franchiser in the United States. Objectives are more specific. Your objectives may include:

- Open your business within the next year.
- Begin to get sales of a specific amount by the end of your second year.
- Hire your first staff person by some particular date.
- Locate and hire the appropriate service professionals (your accountant, attorney, and so forth).

The point is to know where you are going. Be clear. And be results-focused. You want objectives so you can measure your progress as you move toward them.

7. Obstacles. Obstacles are everywhere. They start when your friends and family give you all the reasons why you will fail. Like a spot that won't go away on your favorite suit, obstacles are everywhere. They are the bankers that pass on the opportunity to lend you money and the potential customers that dare to say no to you. For single women, they are the men who walk away from potential relationships because you don't have enough time for them and for married women it's the irritation growing into anger because you know your spouse is suffering as you change the structure of the marriage because—for at least a while—something else has to come first. Obstacles are when your best staff person needs time off for a hysterectomy just when your worst staff person finally (thank God) quits.

Successful women business owners have learned to honestly enjoy obstacles. They thrive on seeing what it takes to get around, over, past, or under each obstacle. They actually enjoy obstacles, although no one wants to admit it.

8. Failure. Women take failure personally. And we are very emotional about it. Can you remember any time when you felt like a failure and didn't cry? When you build a business, lots and lots and lots of things happen that you would not have predicted. Lots of mistakes are made. Someone once said to me that to be a successful business person you needed only to make more right decisions than wrong decisions. In other words, you can make lots of mistakes as long as you have relatively more nonmistakes as time passes.

Know that there is no such thing as failure. There are only lessons to be learned. That has to be your mental attitude for you to play out your potential as an owner of a business. I am not saying that none of you will have to shut down your businesses. Some of you will. The point is to not see this as failing, but as learning how to build a better business next time.

9. Asking for help. Do it. You can probably build a business without any help, but it will take you significantly longer to succeed than it does for those who ask for help and advice along the way. I ask for help from everyone who I think can help me. That way I get the benefit of all their life experiences as well as my own. This doesn't mean that I have to follow anyone else's advice or do everything someone else suggests. Instead, it's a way to create options and weigh the possible consequences of a much wider range of decisions or actions than I could ever have come up with on my own.

10. *Responsibility for your decisions.* As a business owner, you can't blame anyone else for the decisions you make. Ever. When things go wrong, we always want to look around for a scapegoat—an "if only." "If only" the bank had made the loan sooner, we would be profitable this year. "If only" that company president had understood how much our ad campaign would have helped, we'd be swimming in money.

There are no scapegoats for entrepreneurs. All your decisions must be your own. It's a waste of time and energy for you to look for someone else to finger if you make an incorrect decision. You don't have that time and energy to spare. If a decision goes sour, give yourself a pat on the back for making a decision in the first place. Then remember what you now know as a consequence of the decision going sour so it doesn't happen again. And it won't. Women business owners are fast learners with long memories. Something needs to go sour only once. It doesn't happen again.

11. *Total immersion.* Later on I'll talk about balance in your life. It's important over the long haul. But, in the beginning, as I say to my clients, it is the one time in your life where it's fine to be addicted to something (your business). Why? Because you want both your conscious and subconscious mind working for you. The intensity of the focus will help you be creative, optimistic, and full of energy. It will help you to remember all the details of the business and to get done what you need to do, efficiently and effectively. You want to read all the books you can read, go to all the seminars you can afford, and talk to all the entrepreneurs you can about their experiences. You want to learn about planning and marketing and selling and management. You want to be totally immersed in the business in the same way you are immersed in a child the first few months or in a beginning love relationship. The result: a head start.

12. *Ethics.* Never, never compromise your ethical standards. Never. In the end, all you have is your personal reputation. It is built by your honesty and reliability. If you cannot ethically build your business, find a different business. It's that important. As my southern friends put it, "do what's right." You'll know what it is, because women do.

13. *Taking charge*. This is the most fun part of building a business. *You* are the one in charge. You need to like that. All women do, although some of us may not have a great deal of experience in "taking charge" when we first start. This changes quickly. It won't be long before you start saying, "I can do better than that." The rest of us are already talking that way to ourselves. You'll love taking charge.

THE UP SIDE OF ENTREPRENEURSHIP

Which brings me to the up side of owning your own business. There are many wonderful, positive consequences to owning your own business:

- *Excitement*. Women business owners are rarely bored. Most are never bored.

- *Money!* More than 80 percent of women business owners succeed financially. I've been told that women who start service businesses (public relations consulting, human resource work, management assistance, and so forth) triple their income within the first year.

- *Independence*. This is the best news of running your own company. If you want to hold a morning conference call from California to New York in your pajamas, you can do it. If you want to write your client's ad between 8:00 P.M. and 2:00 A.M. and then sleep in, you don't need to ask anyone's permission.

- *Power*. If you didn't have it before, you'll have it as the owner of a business. When you make the decision to start, you owe yourself the gift of going out and getting business cards with your name on them as president of your firm. Then watch how people respond to you in your new role. Presidents of companies are powerful people. Period.

A last up side. Whenever I do a particular seminar for women called "Are You an Entrepreneur?" I always ask the participants to tell me what they think the up side of owning a business will be for them. Twice now, someone in the group has shouted out, "The sex is better." So it must be true.

THE DOWN SIDE OF ENTREPRENEURSHIP

Yes, there is a down side as well and it's important to think through the negative aspects of owning a business:

- *Time.* The first down side is that businesses are time consuming. Like children, they need your undivided attention almost all the time when they are young. Although this gets better as the business matures, you can be sure that the first one to three years will be excruciatingly demanding of your time.

- *Money issues.* More than 90 percent of all businesses need financing from outside sources—mostly banks. In fact, the more successful you are, the more money you will need. Women hate this. I'm not sure why (although I have an idea that it's somehow related to having someone else trying to control us), I just know it's true. It's something you need to learn to live with if you are to build a business.

- *Jerks.* It's always surprising to hear how many women start their businesses to get out from under a miserable boss. Unfortunately, jerk behavior is not the monopoly of poor managers—it can show up anywhere—including in clients. We all have at least one client or customer from hell. Until you learn to fire that person, your life as a business owner could become pretty unhappy. The same truth holds for difficult bankers, suppliers, less-than-good service professionals, and other people close to you who insist on manifesting toxic behavior in your presence.

- *Worse relationships.* I might as well say it now. Most women business owners who are mated end up back in a single state. If you are married, that means divorce. Out of every ten married women business owners I know, only two are still married after several years of business. The mortality rate of relationships is high. While it's true that I have several associates who have purposefully set revenue goals high enough so they can afford to divorce their husbands, they are the exception. Most women want to stay mated. The only way I know to do that is to help your mate to find an obsession of his own (*not* another woman) so he won't notice your absence—like sailing, running, collecting butterflies, cooking. Honest. Getting him involved in your business usually leads to serious problems later on.

So, starting a business is something that you want to discuss at some depth with your mate—before you jump. Sharing a business plan helps. So does talking through the time demands before they hit. At worst, you might want to consider using a good therapist to help you work through the issues together.

WHY IT'S WHAT YOU'LL DO

I've seen it all. I've watched women go out of business. Lose husbands. Face bankruptcy. Lose their best friend. Go through all the negatives. Face the Internal Revenue Service and lose. And every time I've asked them how they felt about the business. I'm that nosy. They told me they'd do it again. Only do it better. With all the downsides, the positive aspects of owning a business far outweighed any emotional or psychological pain they had to endure.

The independence made it all worthwhile. And, like sex, once we've had a taste of what it feels like to take charge, there's no going back.

NETWORKING AS IF YOUR LIFE DEPENDED ON IT

So get help. Get good advice. And get started. Where and how will you find good advice? By networking as if your life depended on it, because it just might. Good networking will reap all sorts of rewards for you: new clients and the team that will help you accomplish your goals.

TEN COMMANDMENTS OF NETWORKING

(From Ivan R. Misner's *Networking for Success*)

1. Have the tools to network with you all the time: a name tag, a card holder full of business cards, and a card file to carry other people's cards.

2. Set a goal regarding how many people you'll meet and don't leave until you've met your goal.

3. Act like a host, not a guest.

4. Exchange business cards with the people you meet.

5. Listen and ask the five "W" questions—who, what, where, when, and why. A notable networker has two ears and one mouth and uses both of them proportionately.

6. Write comments on the back of the business cards you collect. This enables you to remember the person when you follow up the next day.

7. Give a lead or referral whenever possible. If you freely give business to others, they will give business to you.

8. Describe your product or service in sixty seconds. Be specific but brief.

9. Spend ten minutes or less with each person you meet and don't linger with friends and associates. Try not to get caught up in too much idle chatter.

10. Follow up with the people you meet. A simple follow-up letter or telephone call can mean the difference in making the time valuable. If you promise to get back to someone, do it.

Over the next six months you need to identify your professional team (that is, your accountant, attorney, and banker, an industry insider, a mentor, your insurance agent, and your suppliers). If you are already in business and have these professionals, let me ask you this: Do your service professionals feel as if they are on your team? If your answer is no, find a new team. You can't afford to be overlooked or ignored by the very people who are supposed to be helping you to succeed.

The following exercise sheet should help over the next several months. You want to ask every business owner with whom you come into contact whom they use for help. Then ask them to rank them on a scale of one to ten, where ten is the best. Keep a list of the names that get a ranking of eight or better. You will discover that a few names will be mentioned over and over (the cream really does rise to the surface). Go and interview the top three or four:

MY TEAM	NAMES
Accountant	_____
	_____
	_____
	_____
Attorney	_____
	_____
	_____
	_____
Banker (the person, *not* the bank)	_____
	_____
	_____
	_____
Industry expert	_____
	_____
	_____
	_____
Insurance agent	_____
	_____
	_____
	_____
Mentor	_____
	_____
	_____
	_____

For the mentor, I always choose someone I like and trust and who has started a successful business. It needs to be someone of whom you can ask any questions. Why? Because you will fall in love with at least one of your service professionals at some point—your mentor will talk you out of acting on the emotion.

For your accountant, attorney, banker, and insurance agent, I would urge you to make a list of questions you need answered that will tell you how they perform. The following is a beginning checklist for you. Add other questions as you think of them.

For your accountant and attorney:

- Will I have to pay for the initial interview? (Some professionals charge for *every* interview—even the one where you are trying to decide whether even to use them.)

- Do you work with young companies? (If they haven't, *don't* use them.)

- Could you give me some examples?

- Do you know my industry? (If they don't, you need to keep looking.)

- Who will be doing my work? (This is no time to try to save money. It is not okay for a fresh-out-of-school junior accountant or attorney to do your work. I can say that now that I haven't been fresh out of school for years!)

- How accessible are you? (You want someone who will get back to you within twenty-four hours.)

- When do you charge? (You need to know if someone charges you for every ten minutes of work, every telephone call, and so forth. Unfortunately for you, most of us service professional types do charge for pieces of an hour. You also want to know how long it will be before you are billed. The longer the better.)

- What specific services can you offer me? (You will be stunned at the breadth of services provided by attorneys and accountants these days.)

- What are your billing rates? (Brace yourself. The answer will be higher than you ever imagined.)

Last, ask yourself if you both like and trust the person. This is a long-term relationship and the better your service professionals know your goals, style, values, idiosyncrasies, and so forth, the better they will serve you.

The questions for your banker are similar:

- Do you lend to small businesses?
- Do you have women-owned businesses in your portfolio? (If the answer is no, I would find another bank.)
- Do you know my industry?
- What information do you need for a loan?
- What are the parameters of your loans? (For example, what collateral do you need? What are your interest rates? What is the average length of time for this type of loan?)
- With whom will I be working? (Make sure you know this!)
- What is the turnaround on loan decisions?
- Are there other loan programs available through your bank?

Again, it's important to ask yourself if you like and trust the banker you are interviewing, because she will ask you questions you won't want to answer. Also, make sure to meet her boss, because if she is good enough for you to be interviewing her it probably won't be long before she gets promoted and you want her boss to introduce you to her replacement.

The trick to starting a business is to just start. So start. I decided to end this chapter with a quote that has always meant a lot to me. It is a paraphrase of a speech Jill Ruckelshaus made to the National Women's Political Caucus Convention in San Jose in 1977. For some reason, it has always summarized what I want to say to my own clients better than I could ever say it. It is true that "you are in for a very, very long haul. I am asking everything you have to give. Never give up. You will lose your youth, your sleep, your arches, your strength, your patience, your sense of humor . . . and, occasionally, the understanding and support of the people that you love very much. In return, I have nothing to offer you but your pride in being a woman . . . and the certain knowledge that at the end of your days you will be able to look back and say that for once in your life you gave something everything you had."

CHOOSING THE TYPE OF BUSINESS

(or)

IT'S REALLY TRUE THAT IF YOU DO WHAT YOU LOVE THE MONEY WILL FOLLOW

Virtually everyone who doesn't own her own business thinks that those who do knew exactly what they wanted to do before they got started. Wrong. It's a rare woman who knows what type of business she wants to start before she jumps. Even women whose fathers want to bequeath them their businesses (and this is happening more and more!) aren't sure. On average, it takes between six months to a year to think through what it is you want to do.

Where do you start? With your childhood. In a brilliant little book about success (as measured by money—an obsolete but entertaining way to measure success in my view. I'd take free time over money, wouldn't you?), Marsha Sinetar talks about how people who do what they love are successful (that is, they make money). The reason is that the love shows. It creates energy, creativity, and a genuine joie de vivre that is contagious. Now the problem with all us grownups is that we have now spent years doing what other people want us to do and have lives filled with "have-tos" and "shoulds." And we may even have convinced ourselves that we really like this stuff we're doing now. But we don't. At least most of us don't.

As your first step in deciding the type of business to start, you need to remember back to when you were a child and list what you loved to do and what you didn't like to do:

As a child I loved:

_____
_____
_____
_____
_____

As a child I disliked:

_____
_____
_____
_____
_____

Now look at what you wrote down and ask yourself what patterns you see.

_____
_____
_____
_____
_____

Here's an example. When I was a kid, I loved climbing apple trees in my school uniform and throwing the apples at the cows in the field under me. I loved spending a whole day in the woods exploring new trails. I already knew I liked adventure and learning and projects with beginnings and endings. By third grade, I had already figured out how to make money by taking cans of soup, punching holes in them with nails, painting "The Geri

Fund" on them with red nail polish, and putting them by the cash registers in the school cafeteria. All those leftover pennies the other kids didn't want earned me about $12 a week, which in 1957 was a lot of money. Looking back, it is clear that I was on my way to earning my living as someone who would move from project to project in a creative, if in a marginally socially acceptable way. So look at what you wrote down again and pretend you are looking at that child's future and that *there are no rules*. What would that girl be doing now?

_____

_____

_____

_____

_____

Now look at your schooling. List all the classes you can remember taking and categorize them into the ones you loved, the ones you just did with no real reaction, and the ones you hated:

Grade School:

Classes I Loved	Neutral	Classes I Hated
_____	_____	_____
_____	_____	_____
_____	_____	_____
_____	_____	_____
_____	_____	_____

High School:

Classes I Loved	Neutral	Classes I Hated
_____	_____	_____
_____	_____	_____
_____	_____	_____
_____	_____	_____
_____	_____	_____

College:

Classes I Loved	Neutral	Classes I Hated
_____	_____	_____
_____	_____	_____
_____	_____	_____
_____	_____	_____
_____	_____	_____

Now look at your life experiences. What have you tried that you've loved? Examples might be Outward Bound, pottery, baby-sitting, negotiating prices in central American bazaars . . .

_____
_____
_____
_____
_____
_____

What did you hate? If you are anything like me, it was field hockey, an astronomy class (too much detail), and the first six months of aikido.

_____
_____
_____
_____
_____
_____

Now look at what you've written down. What patterns do you see? What does this person like to do?

_____
_____
_____
_____

_____

_____

_____

As a grownup, think of all the different things you do in a day. What are the things you enjoy and what do you dislike?

I Enjoy   I Dislike

_____   _____

_____   _____

_____   _____

_____   _____

_____   _____

_____   _____

Now you can take a deep breath and start narrowing your options. Everyone is good at something. What are you good at?

_____

_____

_____

_____

_____

_____

If you have a hard time with this question, ask your friends. They'll tell you what you're good at. Of these, which do you _love_ doing the most? Another way to ask is this: If you were independently wealthy, what would you do?

_____

_____

_____

_____

_____

_____

What skills are represented in your answer? For example, if you love going to museums, you may have research skills.

Writing is an obvious skill. If you like organizing the family reunions, you have great "operations" skills (that is, you can make things happen).

<u>Skills:</u>

_____
_____
_____
_____
_____
_____
_____
_____

At this point, you should have a pretty good idea of what you're good at, what you love to do, and your skill set. If you've had a tough time with these questions, get a friend or sibling to talk you through them. They can ask you the questions and as you respond, write down your answers for you.

WHAT DO YOU WANT FOR SURROUNDINGS?

The hardest part of your screening is over. The next step is to think hard about the environment you want to create. This is important, because what you sell needs to match your environmental tastes as well. For example, in a management consulting firm such as Deloitte & Touche, we need to be there at least from 8:00 A.M. to 6:00 P.M. because that's what our clients expect. And we need to dress conservatively and formally, because we are advising people about money and they need to feel secure with us. Our offices are very formal and virtually knick-knack free. On the other hand, one of my clients has a health food business. My pearls are out of place there. Instead, the hours are very flexible, even though they work very hard. The dress code is that you need to come clean and clothed. And that's all. No stockings. No ties. No pearls.

What is your style? What environment do you want to be in? Sometimes it's fine to answer this question simply by describing what your office will be like as you visualize it. This is also the time when you want to decide if you want simply to create self-employment for yourself or if you want to hire people, and if so, how many. What about technology—what will you have? Computers, FAXs, interactive videophones? Will you be a consensus-run company or have you waited all your life to be Attila the Hun?

Describe your environment:

_____
_____
_____
_____
_____
_____
_____
_____

The rest of this exercise is great fun. Start skimming all the business-related magazines you find (*Inc.*, *Forbes*, *Fortune*, and so on) and every time you see an article about a company that hits some positive chord in you because it matches your likes, cut out the article and put it in a folder. At the end of a month, pull out the folder and look for patterns:

• What *types* of businesses were you attracted to?

_____
_____
_____
_____
_____
_____

_____

_____

- Which type attracts you the most? Is it a manufacturer of quality toys? Is it a printing franchise? Or a head-hunting firm? Was it an art gallery or a hospice?

Force yourself to choose. You can't do everything. Honest. Lots of us have tried. It doesn't work. Now you are ready for some hard-core library research.

REAL RESEARCH FOR REAL PEOPLE

Once you figure out the type of business you want to start (or if you are already in business, the questions will have been asked as to whether you should stay in the one you have or move on), it's time to find out everything you can about the industry. The best way to do this is to find a library where you can do a database search on the subject—search through periodicals and newspapers to find out everything you can. At a minimum, you want to answer these questions:

- Is this a healthy industry?
- Is it growing?
- What works? (You're after a formula for success here— look for sales and marketing tips, operations ideas like the best computer system to lease, where the hot geographical markets are, and so forth.)
- Who are the gurus? (You never know when you'll need to call.)
- Where are the best locations for this type of business? (You don't want to have a great idea only to find out that it works only in Miami when you are permanently positioned in Wisconsin.)

If your first choice of business is in an industry that isn't growing or is simply in chaos (antiques, banks, etc.), go back over your list of types of businesses and pick a second choice. Do the library research on that. It may take you several tries until you find a business that matches your likes and is in a growing industry. Keep at it. As Baron Rothschild once said, "there are always opportunities."

THE IMPORTANCE OF EXPERIENCE

What if you've chosen a business where you have absolutely no experience? Stop. Go and get the experience in the industry before you do another thing. Why? Because every industry has its own secret ways of doing things that nobody tells you about. It's not that everyone is trying to keep secrets (okay, maybe some people are), it's more that they don't even realize what the unwritten rules are that they're following.

Volunteer if you have to. Just get the experience. Years ago, I had a university professor come into my office—an astrophysicist—who had decided that he had enough of university teaching and wanted to start a Mexican restaurant. He wanted me to help him write a business plan. My ethics are that I won't write one with someone unless I really think they have a shot at success; otherwise, they are spending their money needlessly. It turned out that the gentleman had no restaurant experience, although he was an excellent cook. My advice to him was to go to Mexico for six months to work in a Mexican restaurant. He didn't go. Instead, he opened a Mexican restaurant—and was out of business in six months, because he had no idea how to run a restaurant. Plus, all his university friends kept showing up expecting free food. To his credit, he then spent six months in Texas as an apprentice to a chef and then to the restaurant owner, came back, opened a restaurant sixty miles away (so his friends had to spend time and money to get to him), and last I heard he owned Mexican-food restaurants throughout the Midwest. That is the power of experience in your industry.

YOUR BUSINESS OPTIONS

Starting from Scratch	Buying an Existing Business	Buying a Franchise
Advantages:	Advantages:	Advantages:
Lots of opportunities for innovation	Infrastructure in place	Least amount of risk
Personal fulfillment	Existing clients	Infrastructure already figured out
You get to figure out all the details of the business	May be easiest to finance	Built-in mentors
No baggage from the past		Franchiser may help finance
Disadvantages:	Disadvantages:	Disadvantages:
Riskiest option	Hidden problems you find after you've purchased	Similar to working for someone else in that there are lots of set rules and procedures
	Previous owner may sabotage (create a competitor, etc.)	

WHERE THE MONEY GOES

The franchising industry, by the type of business, 1991.

	SALES (Thousands of Dollars)	Number of Establish-ments
Restaurants (all types)	$ 85,497,411	103,313
Retail (nonfood)	31,384,987	57,035
Hotels, Motels, and Campgrounds	25,384,175	11,398
Business Aids and Services	20,776,567	69,535
Automotive Products and Services	15,460,665	42,222
Convenience Stores	14,992,728	17,265
Retail (food, nonconvenience)	12,175,336	25,378
Rental Services (equipment)	8,037,385	11,113
Real Estate	7,680,265	19,169
Construction, Home Improvements, Maintenance, and Cleaning Services	7,092,670	30,579
Employment Services	6,406,397	8,265
Recreation, Entertainment, and Travel	4,809,233	11,554
Miscellaneous Business Systems	3,787,289	25,288
Educational Products and Services	2,255,005	13,850
Printing and Copying Services	1,969,823	7,422
Rental Services (auto-truck)	771,188	2,898
Tax Preparation	711,732	8,456
Laundry and Dry-Cleaning Services	452,040	3,492
Accounting, Credit, Collection Agencies, and General Business Systems	221,061	1,935
Miscellaneous	2,551,976	8,585
TOTAL	**$232,243,366**	**408,217**

MORE BUSINESS OPTIONS

When you decide that it's time to own your own business, you have several business options. You can start a business from scratch. This is the riskiest option, because you are never positive that there really is a market out there until you open your doors and start to sell. On the other hand, it's the only option where you create something that is totally yours—your vision, your infrastructure, your logo, your company. Or, you can buy an existing business. There is less risk here, because the existing owners have proved that there is a market or they wouldn't still be in business. They may already have found the information and inventory you need and the bank with which you'll work. They will have already created accounting systems, personnel policies, and a marketing and sales strategy (even if it's only in their heads, at least they've thought about it.)

Least risky is purchasing a *high-quality* franchise. Please notice the emphasis on high quality. A synonym here might be reputable. Although it takes some doing to figure out which franchises are the high quality ones, once you've found it your chances of success are better than 80 percent. Reputable franchisers always offer you an operations plan, training, an inventory of products, and marketing help. Some offer financing as well.

FRANCHISES

The best way to think about a franchise is to imagine a store owned by an individual with a unique concept. The Body Shop is an example. Another might be Merle Norman. If the business is really successful, as both of these have been, the owner may develop a second or third store and hire employees for the day-to-day operations of the store. At that point, if the owner still wants to expand but prefers not to own and operate additional stores herself, she may decide to "franchise" her store name and business system. So, she sells the right to use her name, business system (that is, how she pulls everything together), and the right to own a store using the name and system (in legal terms called a license) to someone else (in legal terms called the franchisee).

In return, she gets a start-up fee and a continuing royalty payment based on some percentage of the franchisee's sales.

This is a business system that works very well in the United States. There are more than 2,000 franchises available to you as I write. While it's true that many are the old-fashioned types— truck and car dealerships, gas stations, and soft drink bottlers— more and more are service and retail businesses.

You can buy the right to businesses ranging from Duds 'n' Suds, a laundry/singles bar based in Ames, Iowa, to Molly Maid, a cleaning franchise where service staff wear English maids' uniforms.

In the early 1990s, the fastest growing franchises are expected to be:

- Fast-food restaurants

- Rental services

- Employment agencies

- Printing-related businesses

- Hotels, Motels

- Specialty clothing stores

What are the costs of franchising? According to the September 1987 issue of *Black Enterprises*, franchise costs ranged from $6,000 to close to $1 million:

WHAT ARE THE COSTS OF FRANCHISING?

McDonald's	$350,000
Kentucky Fried Chicken (KFC)	$620,000–$820,000
Wendy's	$750,000–$1.3MM
Subway Sandwiches	$ 29,900–$60,000
Hallmark Cards	$ 55,000
Meineke Discount Muffler Shop	$ 48,500
American Speedy Printing Centers	$ 30,000
Lawn Doctor, Inc.	$ 30,000
Molly Maid	$ 18,000–$21,000
National Maintenance Contractors	$ 1,500–$20,000

Although time will have changed these prices to some extent, now you have a ball-park idea of what you need to save.

If you are interested in franchising, the best help you can give yourself is to order a "Franchise Opportunities Handbook" from the International Franchise Association. The address is 1025 Connecticut Avenue N.W., Suite 707, Washington, DC 20036. The cost is under $10.

The handbook lists the names of more than a thousand franchises, as well as:

- Brief description of their operation,
- How many franchises they have,
- The year they started,
- How much money you need to come up with to be a franchisee,
- Whether the franchiser will lend you money toward the franchise,
- Whether training and managerial assistance is available.

Every Thursday, *The Wall Street Journal* focuses on franchise opportunities, doing the best job it can to screen possible fly-by-nights. Remember that even the *Journal* can't be perfect. The trick is to follow the ads for several weeks; fly-by-nights usually can't afford to run an ad in a major paper for a long time. *Inc.* magazine also lists franchise ads and regularly has a whole section on franchising and franchisers. Franchising trade shows are always going on somewhere. They'll give you an opportunity to meet the franchiser and/or her staff face-to-face.

When you discover a franchiser that matches what you want to do, research it in as much depth as you can:

1. Write for all the materials they've developed for prospective franchisees.

2. Find out the type of experience they require.

3. Find out what commitment you would need to make to successfully run a franchise (money, time, people).

4. Find out what products and/or services you would have to purchase as a part of your agreement and how and by whom they will be supplied.

5. Talk to other franchisees to find out how they have done and whether the franchiser has truly been helpful. My favorite question is, "Would you do it again?"

It may take a dozen tries before you find a franchise that suits you. Once you find it, pay the cost of obtaining the legal agreement and get an attorney to review it with you. An accountant may be helpful in putting together your financial projections so you will know what to expect if you purchase the franchise.

By that point, you'll have a gut feeling of whether or not the franchise will work for you. If it will, in the words of Nike, "*Just do it!*"

BUYING AN EXISTING BUSINESS

There are several ways to find an existing business that might be for sale. Oftentimes, they are advertised on the weekends in the business opportunity section of the local newspapers. *The Wall Street Journal* carries ads for businesses for sale. So do regional weekly business magazines such as *Crain's*. I just start asking. I ask my accountant and ask her to ask all of her associates. I ask my banker and ask her to send a memo around to her colleagues in local branch offices. I talk to lawyers. Realtors might know. I tell all my business owner friends I'm on the hunt. At worst, you can put your own ad in a local paper describing the type of business you are looking for and where you would like it to be.

The trick to deciding about existing businesses is figuring out what the real story is. *Why* is the owner selling? You need to know before you make any decisions. Many owners want to get rid of a business that is going downhill. Unfortunately, they can be very good at hiding the going downhill part until you've signed a sales agreement. So get the facts. All of them. Is she selling because she's tired? Because there is no one to pass the company to? Because her partner just left? Why? Why? Why? Don't stop researching this question until you know—in your gut—that you've figured out the reason.

Some advisers say that it's fine to buy a business going downhill if it has a market. They'll tell you you can turn it around with your energy, skills, and determination. I disagree. Buying a business that is on a downhill roll is like starting a marathon a mile behind everyone else. Maybe you'll catch up, but why go through the extra pain when you don't need to. In their book *The Woman's Guide to Starting a Business,* Claudia Jessup and Genie Chapps offer an excellent checklist for women researching existing businesses. In it they cover issues like finding hidden debt and how long it really takes for customers to pay and whether there are any zoning laws you should know about. (There usually are.)

I look for businesses that are chugging along just fine but for personal reasons the owner wants out. You'll have enough headaches with a good business—you don't want to get carried away with trying to solve infrastructure, location, people, or major marketing issues.

Once you've identified the business you want to buy and you've had an accountant look through the books and an attorney look for any legal problems, it's time to talk price.

Business valuation is an art, not a science. There are no magic mathematical formulas that will tell you what to pay for a business. It's more a question of judgment on the part of you and your accountant. When businesses are valued, several fundamental factors of the business are always evaluated:

- The nature of the business and its history.
- The economic outlook—both for the economy as a whole and for the industry the business is in.
- The tangible assets of the company (that is, any buildings, vehicles, machinery, furniture, inventory, or other fixtures). Any cash in the bank. Any receivables.
- The financial history of the company (have they always paid their bills promptly, have their customers paid their bills promptly, and so forth), any liabilities, any credit problems, what the balance sheet looks like.
- "Goodwill." This is subjective and has to do with the reputation of the company—if its customers, suppliers, bankers all love it, then you'll be paying something here. If they don't, you won't need to pay for "goodwill."
- The situation of comparable companies.

The seller will always have an asking price. Your job is to decide if it's fair or if you want to make a counter offer based on what you've found out researching the firm and the industry. Get help from an accountant and an attorney on this. Once you figure out the price you want to pay, just pretend you're buying a house and keep negotiating back and forth until you come to an agreement you both accept.

YOUR OWN BUSINESS

Most women discover that they can't find an existing business to buy that matches their tastes and values. More are finding franchises that will work for them. Most decide simply to go out on their own. That's what you will probably do. Before you make any permanent business decisions, your first task is to name this baby. Now, names are not as easy as they first appear to be. There are many examples of how names have gotten in the way of company or product success. Here's just one example. When I was in Portugal last spring, I got to talking to some Portuguese businessmen about which American products they buy and which they don't. It turns out that the Pinto car, which was very popular in the rest of Europe, had a tough time in Portugal. It turns out that Pinto is slang for "tiny penis." There was no way these gentlemen, who are already fairly short relative to other men, were going to buy a car named "Pinto." Life is already tough enough.

There is actually a specific process for naming companies. The one I use with my clients was taken from the Salinon Corporation's "The Naming Guide: How to Choose a Winning Name for Your Company, Service or Product."

The process works equally well for a company or a product. Here are the steps:

1. *Describe what you are naming.* What are your business's key features and characteristics? What are your advantages over your competitors?

2. *Decide what you want the name to do for you.* Do you want it to convey a certain image the way names like Nutech (new technology) or L'Oreal (French, elite, sensuous) do? Do you want people to have a certain image of your company? An example here is "Two Men and a Truck," a successful bare bones trucking company in Michigan.

3. *Figure out who you want your name to appeal to.* What type of people? What type of companies?

4. *Start a list of names you really like and names you really dislike.* Don't stop until you have a hundred of each. When you're done, analyze your reactions. What is it about names that makes you like them? What do they have in common? Are

they short? Foreign? Female sounding? Are there certain roots or phrases that strike your fancy? Or ones that you dislike? I usually circle the ones I like best and brainstorm more like them. Then I pick my five or six favorites and go on with the process, making sure they're all easy to pronounce and look good in print.

5. *Compare your choices with your competitors' names.* Which ones stand out in a positive way? This should narrow your choice to two or three names.

6. *Check your names out for possible off-color meanings.* Since I'm based in the state that is home to GM, Chrysler, and Ford, my name examples tend to be related to cars. Take the "Probe" car for example. It took me two years before I saw a woman driving one on the highway. It's actually a great car for women, but if most of you are like me and my friends, every time we heard the word "probe," we had visions of our gynecologist's office—not a happy thought. Who wants to have a flash of her gynecologist's office when she gets into her car? No one I know.

7. *Check with your State Department of Commerce to make sure someone else doesn't already have the name.* You would be surprised at how many of us come up with the same names for our company. The (insert your last name here) Group is probably taken already; so is (insert your name here now) and Associates or The (insert your name one more time) Company.

8. *Finally, try out your name on potential customers to see how they respond.* Do they like it? Do they think it matches your company? Does it remind them of something you want them to be reminded of? What images or connotations do they associate with the name when they hear it? Are they positive? See if they can remember the name when you mix it up with others. If they like the name, it conjures

up positive associations and they can remember it, go register it. If not, start over until you get the reactions you want.

So be careful in choice to names. It is worth the investment of time to discover the right one.

CHAPTER 3

*Y*OUR FIRST

(AND MOST IMPORTANT)

BUSINESS

DECISIONS

Ignorance of the law does not equate to innocence.
Every U.S. Judge That Ever Lived

By the time you have figured out what type of business you want to start, you should have also identified your accountant and attorney. If you haven't, this is the time. Why? Because you are about to make permanent decisions related to the business.

The first one has to do with partnerships. Do you want to start your business alone or with someone else? Most women want partners. In fact, one of my best friends has a great business idea that she's been holding onto for two years waiting until she's found the right partner. To me, that's like waiting to live your life fully until you've found the right mate. (Is this making sense to you or am I the only woman in America who enjoys taking cruises by herself?)

JUST SAY NO TO PARTNERSHIPS

I don't like partnerships. Even a little. Most management consultants tell you that you will be either a creative person or a managerial-type person and what you want to do is find the missing half in someone else. In my experience, this never works (well, okay, maybe twice—but that's in a population pool of hundreds of businesses). Here's why it doesn't work. You always end up in a huge fight. Huge. Most often a dish or folder-throwing drag-out "you were the one who screwed up" fight. If you are two women working together, I think it's that your monthly cycles get closer and closer until you start hitting PMS at the same time—which creates all sorts of problems (women who work closely with lots of other women know exactly what I mean). If your partner is a man, he will tell you how to do something (not that you asked for his opinion) one time too many. And it's all over. Breaking up partnerships is as painful as any divorce—and sometimes worse. Which brings me to mates. Many women look to their mates as partners. While it's true that the country is populated with Mom'n'Pop businesses, most of them were started in the olden days when men called all the shots (you know, until 1991 or so). Go see for yourself. Businesses started by husbands who bring in their wives as the office help are a very different breed from businesses started by the wife. Except for three businesses I can think of where the wife calls all the shots (and that's what makes it work), here are three reasons why you should never be in a partnership with your husband or mate:

1. You'll probably have to fire him at some point. The more successful women become, the harder it is on their mates—unless they are keeping up. And there's no way your mate can keep up with you if he's working for you. (A side comment here—in my experience, Lesbian partnerships do tend to work; I wish some academic

would try to discover all the reasons why. I think we could all benefit.) Firing a mate usually results in a dissolution of the relationship.

2. If you are both intimately involved in the business, you can never get away from it. It's what you think and talk about during the day and what you think and talk about at night. Even when you try not to, the business sort of seeps into everything. The result is psychological fatigue, a loss of your creative juices, and in the end, burnout on both your parts. Which can also lead to divorce.

3. By having your spouse actively involved in the business, you are losing a valuable "outside" opinion of your activities. You want other world views from which you can bounce your ideas and strategies.

If you are creative, you can buy the management side of your business in the form of your service professionals (attorney and accountant), a board of advisers, and the staff you hire. If you are a "managerial" type, just give yourself some time. You won't believe how creative you can be once you are in your own business.

IF YOU STILL INSIST

If after all these problems you still insist on a partnership, here's how to find one. First, figure out what you are looking for in terms of skills. Do you want someone who loves detail, is a numbers woman, lives to sell, what? Then, tell everyone you know what you are looking for. Tell your friends, neighbors, associates, banker, attorney, accountant. Tell your hairdresser (you won't believe the network he or she has). See if there is someone working for a competitor ready to make the leap to independence. Once you've found someone who is a match, interview her over and over and over and over. Visit her in her environment. Find out how she functions under stress.

If the person passes your test, you need to write a partnership agreement. In it, you need to spell out:

- Your job descriptions, including who is responsible for doing what and what authority to make decisions each of you has. For example, can you both write checks for the business? Order supplies? Decide when to put an ad in the paper?

- How much ownership you each have. This is not as easy as it sounds. What if one of you invests more money in the company than the other one? What if one of you brings clients with you? Or a contract? What if one of you has the actual skill set that you'll be selling? You need to talk about this until you each feel as if you have an agreement that's fair to both of you. A good place to start is where both of you own 50 percent. Then, let each of you make a case for why this *isn't* the right proportion. If you can't come to an agreement on this topic, the partnership will never work. Go find a different partner or decide to go it alone.

- How will you resolve disagreements? Even though right now it may seem as though you think exactly alike—just wait. There are always disagreements. And that can be healthy as long as you've figured out how to resolve them. My rule of thumb is that only one person can be president at a time. Even if you each name yourselves principal or have some other egalitarian title, you need a tie-breaker function.

- What are your buy-and-sell arrangements for when one of you decides it's time to move on?

- Who is someone that you both agree can act as a mediator should you come to something that appears to be unresolvable? As I write, I know I'm sounding overly concerned, but all it takes is seeing two gorgeous petite co-partners in a fist-fight over an issue to convince a person that these issues need to be resolved at the front end of a partnership.

Once you've decided whether to go it alone or bring in a partner, you need to formally choose a legal structure. Although there are many structure choices, most women start out as *individual proprietors*. Basically, this means that you are the business. No government approval is needed, although I would always check with local, county, state, and even federal agencies to see if you need any special licenses. As one example, a wonderful Detroit woman started a pie company several years ago in her house. She soon found that there were all sorts of rules and regulations related to making food that you sell to the public. So ask. Then ask again. Not knowing that you need a license or that there's some regulation you have to follow is no protection.

Where to get licenses and other legal documents you need to file:

DOCUMENTS

You need many documents for your business. Some are:

- a License to Do Business
- a Certificate of Partnership
- documents related to Zoning Regulations
- a Seller's Permit (Sales Tax for Resale Number for Retailers)
- Health/Safety Requirements, and
- information regarding taxes

Most of these can be found at a county clerk's office or at a local IRS or Department of Labor office.

If you use your own name for your business, you just need to get some business cards, an address (more on this later), a telephone number, and some stationery and you are in business. To my knowledge, in most states if you are using a different name for your business you need to file a dba (doing business as) form at the city or county level. In Ann Arbor, I can just walk down to the county courthouse, plunk down $15, name a company, provide some personal information about myself such as my home address, swear that everything I have said is true and voila: a business is born. Legally, the real ramification of a sole proprietorship is that all your business profits are taxed as your personal income—both on the federal and usually on the state and local levels. You are responsible for paying federal self-employment (FICA) tax, so you'll get social security (assuming there's some left by the time we're ready for it!).

If you've insisted on creating a formal partnership in spite of all my warnings, you will need to file a dba and to write out a formal partnership agreement. Some states require that you file something called a Certificate of Conducting Business as Partners and some don't. Call your county clerk to find out. In partnerships, *each partner* is responsible for all the debts and taxes of the business. The way this works is as follows: Your accountant will help you to file an income tax return that summarizes how the business did that year—including how much you made and any losses you might have incurred. Then you treat the income and losses as your own and pay the tax or get the credits.

CORPORATIONS

Then there are corporations. To incorporate, you create a business by filing articles of incorporation with your state. These articles normally include:

- The name of the company.
- The location of your headquarters.
- What the business is all about.
- The names and addresses of all the owners of the business (including anyone you've given stock to).
- The type of stock you are issuing.
- How much stock you are issuing.
- How much money is being invested in the business to get it started.

Get an attorney to help you file. Since a corporation is a legal entity that goes on and on until you formally dissolve it (which costs money), a good attorney can help you make wise decisions about ownership, stock, and so forth, from the beginning. If you want to save some money on legal fees, you can ask your attorney in advance what will be all the information she will need from you, which you can then take to her to translate into legalese and to file. Deciding whether to incorporate is a serious decision. My advice is that most women do best starting out as a sole proprietorship until they know for sure what they want to do.

There are lots and lots of rules related to corporations. Worse, they are always changing. To try to review them all here would be a boring and painful exercise for both of us; get your attorney to give you a summary of what you need to know or watch for a class on legal decisions for entrepreneurs at your local community college or Chamber of Commerce. Someone is always sponsoring a seminar on this somewhere. The main decision you need to make regarding corporations is whether you even want to be one. If you are planning to hire employees, handle a controversial product (such as hazardous waste dumping), or think that your customers will have a penchant for suing you, a corporation is probably a good idea. Then you need to decide type: whether you want to be an S Corporation or a C Corporation. This is a fairly complicated decision. There are advantages and disadvantages to each. Basically, an S Corporation is a company that is considered to be closely held. In other words, there are very few owners (usually just you). Because of that, the corporation's taxes flow through to you. In other words, the corporation doesn't pay taxes; it pays you a profit on which you are then taxed. You are treated as one and the same thing. That's the good news—you don't get double taxed. On the other hand, if someone gets mad at the corporation and decides to sue it, they'll sue you. In other words, there's no protection of your personal assets in an S Corporation. In a C Corporation there is more protection, because a C Corporation really is its own entity. However, because it is its own entity, you'll pay taxes twice. The choice between these two forms is personal. It depends on your situation, the type of business you are starting, whether you have a lot of personal assets you want to protect, and how lawsuit-happy people are in your area. Take time to figure out the pros and cons of each and then decide. If it turns out that you've made the wrong choice, you can change it later.

THE PRESENT ADVANTAGES AND DISADVANTAGES OF DIFFERENT STRUCTURES

Be advised that these could change with every new administration in Washington and sometimes in between.

- **Individual Proprietorship**

    <u>Advantages</u>:
    Low start-up costs.
    Greatest freedom from regulation.
    Owner in direct control.

Minimal working capital requirements.
No separate income tax returns required.
All profits available to owner.
Simplest to form.
Owner may take action without delay or other
formalities.

Disadvantages:
Unlimited personal liability.
Lack of continuity.
Difficulty in raising capital.
Fewer opportunities for tax advantages.

- **General Partnership**

Advantages:
Ease of formation.
Low start-up costs.
Additional sources of venture capital, labor property
and/or skills.
Broader management base.
Possible tax advantages.
Limited outside regulation.

Disadvantages:
Unlimited liability.
Lack of continuity.
Divided authority.
Difficulty in raising capital.
Difficulty in finding suitable partners.

- **Corporation**

Advantages:
Limited liability (although shareholders in a small
corporation may be required to assume individual
liability in such areas as obtaining capital or

nonpayment of taxes).
Specialized management.
Transferable ownership.
Continuous existence.
Separate legal entity.
Greater opportunities for tax advantages.
Capital easier to raise.

Disadvantages:
Closely regulated.
Most expensive form to organize.
Extensive record-keeping necessary.
Corporation taxes in addition to the individual owners'.
Corporation losses usually not available to owners.

- **S Corporation**

  A special type of corporation, the S Corporations may be
  taxed as if it were a general partnership because the losses
  and profits flow through to the individual shareholders
  for tax purposes, just as losses or income flow through to
  partners for tax purposes. If a corporation qualifies (typically by having thirty-five or fewer shareholders), its income will be taxed to the shareholders. "S" status usually
  avoids the corporate income tax, and corporate losses can
  be claimed by the shareholders. However, undistributed
  taxable income is subject to the maximum individual income tax rates.

INSURANCE DECISIONS

The decisions aren't over yet. There are all kinds of insurance
decisions related to starting a business: building insurance, stuff
in the building insurance, rent insurance, health and life insurance, liability insurance if you think you'll have customers

who will decide to sue you. (The reality of the 1990s, unfortunately, is that all of us will need some form of liability insurance. Maybe it's because our sisters all became lawyers and they need work. Maybe it's because of all the stories we hear of juries awarding huge settlements to wronged customers. The point is that you need protection.) The trick here is to find an insurance agent you can trust, one who has been around for a while and who knows the needs of emerging businesses. Then listen to what she tells you.

Don't start a business without insurance. For those of you who are building a business around a manufactured product such as a children's toy, I'll make my words stronger. *Don't do anything* until you make certain that you can get liability insurance and that you can afford the costs. I've watched several companies with good products go out of business in the first year because they were never able to find liability insurance they could afford. So be careful not to waste your time on products you'll never be able to take to the street.

Don't be afraid to ask your agent if there are ways to save money on your insurance. For example, you may be able to get group insurance through the local Chamber of Commerce, your industry group, or an association of women business owners such as the National Association of Women Business Owners (NAWBO). Or you may get a cheaper policy if you are willing to pay a higher deductible. Put another way, if you are willing to cover a higher amount up front, then your monthly insurance costs could end up being significantly lower. Just be sure that you're fully covered so that you really could replace everything through insurance if you had to.

While you're at it, it's not a bad idea to have your insurance agent do a walk-through of your business and potential space (before you rent or buy it) to look for potential problem areas. One of my clients has a five-year lease in a lovely building. I think the building was constructed by trolls. All the steps are about two inches shorter than a normal step. The result: *everyone* trips walking into her office. Even those of us who know about "the step problem" trip. For me, it's every time. If she had known to have her insurance agent go through the space before she rented it, she wouldn't be there today. She's just too liable. All she needs is one good fall on the part of one of her customers and she could lose the business.

FORMS, FORMS, FORMS

You need to fill out special forms for the IRS to get an employer identification number. Beyond that, you will have state forms to fill out as well. Remember that ignorance of the law is no protection. That means it is your responsibility to track down all the forms you need to fill out. Your accountant will help identify the forms. There will be state forms and there may be city and county forms to be completed. The point is to find them and fill them out or get your accountant to do it for you if you can't do it alone. Before you start beating yourself up for not understanding the forms, know that you aren't alone. We're all confused. So get help. Spend the money. It's one of those sanity protectors you'll need as you grow the company. Also, make certain to ask your accountant to list for you all the times when you'll need to make a tax payment to someone somewhere—then post it where you won't forget to check it. And don't assume that just because you aren't making money you won't have to pay taxes. It isn't true. You'll need to pay taxes ranging from sales taxes, to specialty taxes, payroll taxes, no matter your income. So protect yourself—and don't be tempted to use money you are saving for taxes for something else. This is beyond dangerous; it can be deadly. In business, you can't rob Peter to pay Paul and live to tell about it. When you don't pay the IRS their due, not only do they come after you, they also charge significant interest on what you owe them. Every year I hear of at least one company that's out of business because the owner used the money she had saved for taxes to pay a supplier or payroll. It's better to go without the suppliers. Or the employees. As I think about it, just about anything is less painful than having to deal with an irritable IRS, state, or city tax agent. Ugh.

FUN DECISIONS: LOCATION, LOGOS AND LOCAL AREA NETWORKS

You need a computer. Go lease one. And then if you like it, buy one like it. Most of my smaller clients (one to ten employees) have Macintoshes; most of my larger clients have IBM PCs. It's a personal decision. Let me just say, you'll need one because you'll be tracking all sorts of information: financial data, sales data, mailing list information, and so forth. Trying to track data manually isn't something for which you'll have time. So it's critical to find a computer to love and use. And make sure it's one you'll be able to network to other computers as your staff increases in size.

You also need a work space, one where you can close a door, leaving the rest of your life behind you. When my sister started her own CPA practice in order to spend more time with her preschoolers, she would get up in the morning, get dressed for work, wait for her baby-sitter to get to the house, kiss her kids good-bye, walk out the front door, around the house and into the back door, and down to the basement, where she would spend up to six hours a day in her home-based office. It was the perfect arrangement. She was right there, so she could join her kids for lunch and be home early, yet she made herself "go to work" so she could physically separate her wife-and-mother role from her business owner role. It was a system that worked.

Futurists are telling us that up to a quarter of all workers now work at home. Most of them are women who own their own businesses. I say they're on to something. The last thing you want to spend money on is rent to someone else. Plus, if you have a bona fide home office and you can prove it (go to your accountant for this too), there are *great* tax advantages. So stay home if you can. Now, everyone else will probably try to talk you out of what I'm saying, telling you that you'll feel isolated and spend a lot of time running around to printers, getting letters typed, and so forth that you wouldn't have to do if you had an office nearer to everything. Here's my response: My happiest years were when I could wake up at 5:00 A.M., walk down the hall to my office, produce a report in my pajamas while drinking a Diet Coke, and go back to bed for a quick nap at 11:00 A.M. when I finished. It just doesn't get better. If you need a fancy office in which you can meet clients, go rent one by the hour from a fancy office building (they need all the help they can get right about now!) or join a fancy club where you have access to fancy meeting rooms. If you don't, at worst you can have all your business meetings in restaurants over a meal.

The only exception to this rule is retail space. Even manufacturing can usually be done in your basement at first. You would be amazed at the things I've seen manufactured in basements or garages—just about everything up to a car or an entire house. On the other hand, people tend to be unwilling to go to a person's home to buy retail products (unless you hold product parties for makeup, toys, condoms, lingerie, and things like that). Plus, retail spaces need to be where your customers are: on the correct downtown street, in the correct mall, on the right corner. Get help from a savvy (honest) business realtor if you are looking for a retail space—she will save you significant research time.

And for God's sake, don't buy any plants or new furniture (unless it's a portable work station made by Joy Naylor at JNV Associates in Ann Arbor. Her work stations look like trundle beds, but they unfold to a large comfortable desk, work station and bookcase for when you need it. Call her at 313-663-4666. Don't buy pictures, new rugs, or shelves. Why? Because you are spending your money on the wrong things. In the beginning of a business, you should be putting every penny into the things that will help you to get and track sales: your computer, advertising, product supplies, a bookkeeping system or person, more advertising, car money, and stamps.

One of these expenses is your logo, which you then want to integrate into a letterhead. Unless you are about to make your way in the world as a self-employed consultant (in which case you only need a nice business card and personal stationery), you need a logo. It makes your company appear to be large, stable, and permanent to everyone with whom you'll be working. This is an important—and fun—decision. The place to start is to begin collecting logos that really appeal to you. Keep a folder. Then, when you get to somewhere around a hundred samples, pick the ten that appeal to you the most and figure out why. Are they pictures or words or symbols? Are they delicate or strong? In bright colors or black and white? Are they bold or subtle?

Once you've analyzed what you like about the logos, find a graphic artist that you like (the process is identical to finding your accountant and attorney). Pay for her time to listen to you describe your business, your vision for the business, and what you like about the logos you chose. Then have her create three to five logos for you that you can then show to anyone who will look and ask them which one best suits your business. Usually, one or two stand out. If you like either of them—you have a logo! If you don't, go back to the graphic artist and have her repeat the process with you until a logo emerges that people chose and that *you like*. Spend the time and the money to get it right. Remember, you will be using it for the life of your business.

Once you have your logo, put it everywhere you can afford. It needs to be on your stationery and business cards. You can put it on your car on one of those big magnetic stickers that you can slap on when you are doing business and take off when you are going on a date. You can put your logo on the Post-its™ you use to send notes to customers, you can turn it into a pin that you can wear everywhere. You can put it on baseball caps, clothes, notebooks, duffel bags, folders, gift cards, and on the product itself. Don't be shy. The more people see your logo, the more they'll remember you and what you are trying to do, and that's exactly what you want to happen.

The last business decision in this first group has to do with who will be answering your telephone. Now, I know we are living in a hi-tech age. And that we all have answering machines. And most of us are comfortable communicating via modem. On the other hand, I also know that consumers are hungry to be treated as individuals, with respect, in a personalized way.

What does all this mean to you when you are starting a business? It means this: Get a real person to answer your telephone. So far most consumers I know dislike voice mail intensely. We're tired of answering machines. We don't want to hold a conversation with a computer either. When we want to buy a product or service, we want to talk to a real person. Someone who is friendly and cares about us. Someone who knows something about the product being sold. Someone who honestly wants us to be satisfied. That someone could be your mother. (This is the *only* job to offer her.) Or a retired person who is willing to take calls for you. Or a reputable answering service. Or you whenever you have time. Use an electronic system, like an answering machine, only as an emergency backup.

Remember, part of the reason why women are starting businesses that are succeeding at three to five times the rate of male-owned businesses is that *we take care of our customers. We care.* An answering machine doesn't care. A voice mail system doesn't care. Only a person can care. And your customers know it.

CHECKLIST FOR STARTING A BUSINESS

☐ Decide your business's legal structure.

☐ Register your business name.

☐ Obtain any special licenses you need.

☐ Arrange for registration and payment of federal taxes.

☐ If you need a state sales tax license, get it.

☐ Decide whether your business will hire employees and, if it will, go get the appropriate forms.

CHAPTER 4

MONEY ISSUES:

CREATING A BUDGET SYSTEM
THAT WORKS FOR YOU

*Inflation is the process that enables you to live in a more expensive
neighborhood without going to the trouble of moving.*
A. W. Claussen, President, Bank of America

We hate dealing with money. It's not that we mind spending
it. What gets us is trying to figure out how much we have or
need and tracking it. For many of us, our mothers never
balanced their checkbook because it was the husband's job. (In
the case of my mother, each child took a turn trying to keep her
checkbook balanced. When we had to give up—which usually
took as little as two months' time—we would pass the task on
to another sibling until all five of us had tried. Then we'd start
the process over. To this day, I'm afraid to look at her checkbook
to see the shape it's in. And she's a smart, savvy woman!)

It's time, don't you think, to get rid of our antiquated views
of money—that it's dirty, or it means we've sold ourselves, that
we don't deserve it, that we won't have it. Money is simply a
tool. That's all. It helps us to take our businesses where we want
them to go. No more. No less. It's not something to obsess over
any more than are youth or the gorgeous young salesman who
sold you this book. It just is. Don't let it be more than that or
you'll make poor financial decisions.

Start with your personal checkbook. You need to know how
to balance it. If you don't, have someone teach you. I paid a

woman from my credit union $7 an hour to teach me this fine art. And whenever I get too creative (You'll know when this happens. You'll either have $300 too much or $300 too little in your checking account, but you won't be certain which one is true.), I pay her to review the rules with me.

DEVELOPING A CREDIT HISTORY

The next step in getting your financial house in order is to develop a credit history if you don't already have one. One of the ironies of the business world is that you are *penalized for paying with cash*. Here's what I mean by that. The people who make up your financial relationships, your banker, suppliers, investors, will all want to see proof that you know how to borrow money and pay it back. They want to see credit purchases in your past. Again and again. If you were raised that borrowing is bad, you need to unlearn the lesson. Not only will you need to borrow money for your business, you will need to borrow money before you will be taken seriously as an entrepreneur.

How? Get credit cards. In your own name. Use them. Finance a car. Get a house. Buy appliances over time. Use a charge card to purchase clothing. The point is to establish a record of borrowing and paying money back. As long as you know how to pay your bills, you can't do too much of this. Once you get the hang of it, this is really a fun game. The only exception is if you are a woman who has trouble paying off debts. In that case, be very careful. You might want to stick with one debt at a time until you feel secure paying money back.

MONITORING YOUR CREDIT RATING

The track record you are establishing by borrowing for your car, using credit cards, and so forth, is stored in the form of a credit report. We each have one. TRW, Equifax and TransUnion are huge firms that keep almost all of our records. Because your success as an entrepreneur will first depend on having a good credit rating, it's important to find out what your credit report says about you.

First, I want to review some rights you have as a woman. Although you will be too young to remember this, prior to 1974 women had a terrible time getting credit. We couldn't get our own credit cards or borrow money for cars on our own. A woman who was able to obtain her own mortgage became instantly famous in her circle of associates. It was awful.

THE EQUAL CREDIT OPPORTUNITY

Then, in 1974, the Equal Credit Opportunity Act was passed. It flat-out prohibited discrimination against anyone on the basis of sex, color, religion, age, or marital status. I would like to believe that your creditors are all aware of the act and behave accordingly, but my experience has shown that a surprising number of sources of credit, especially small, young companies, aren't aware of the law.

You need to know your rights. Here are the main ones:

- You have a legal right to establish your own credit.
- If you are denied credit, you have the right to find out why.
- You can't be refused credit just because:
  - You are female.
  - You are single.
  - You are married. (This one is tricky. You aren't really protected if your spouse has lousy credit because he insisted on VISAing that camcorder when your budget was tight. Since there are circumstances where you may

need a co-signature from a spouse or his credit record, he needs to be good at paying bills, too.)

- You are separated or divorced.

- You are a widow.

- You can't be refused credit because a creditor thinks you're the right age to have a baby and if you do your business will go to hell in a hand basket. (This would be funny if it didn't happen, but it does.)

There are more provisions of the law that you might want to review. The Governors of the Federal Reserve System (Washington DC 20551) have a terrific pamphlet that more completely summarizes your rights under the act. Learn them. Unfortunately, you may need them.

Once you've been charging, you'll have a track record. You want to find out how the credit-reporting agencies are describing that track record before they send it off to anyone else.

Why? Because there will be mistakes on it. Think about it. These credit companies are continually getting pieces of information about all of us millions of consumers. The person who is inputting the information into their mega-database is sitting there hour after hour inputting data. It is not her job to check the existing information for accuracy. In fact, it's no one's job. Now think of the number of typos you make when you are simply typing out information that doesn't mean anything personal to you. Get the picture?

I order my credit report every couple of years just to see what is being said about me, and I have yet to receive a completely accurate report. The first time I had a notice on my report that I still owed a hospital in Portland, Oregon, about $1,000 from when I gave birth to my son more than ten years ago. Not only was the information wrong, but by law, information that old isn't even supposed to be in the report. My understanding is that after seven years you have the right to get rid of information you don't want on the report. The second time I discovered a whole series of comments about being a slow-payer, which in the credit world is almost as bad as not paying. I hadn't realized that paying my credit card bills at the last minute would have that consequence. Now I pay a week sooner—to be safe.

The third time there was a loan from a bank in Des Moines, Iowa. Although I'm looking forward to my first trip to Des Moines, I haven't been there yet and don't know a single banker. But *I* had to prove that I never had that loan to get it off my report.

The last time was when I applied for a mortgage for my house. My banker, who is also a friend, called me to tell me that the loan committee had turned me down flat. The reason—my credit report. It turned out that a woman with my exact name was buying houses in Detroit and charging appliances for them. She would rent the house for a while and when it got too dilapidated she would abandon it, stop paying for appliances, and move on to the next house—apparently using *my* good credit rating to get the new appliances. That one took all sorts of letters and comparisons of social security numbers to clean up. The moral of the story is that you need to see your credit report before anyone else does.

OBTAINING A COPY OF THE REPORT

How do you get it? My approach is to call your local telephone operator and ask for the nearest TRW office. If there isn't one nearby, ask for Equifax or TransUnion. You will get a recorded message from them that tells you how to obtain your report. Usually, the choice is either to go to their office in person or to send a letter formally requesting a copy of your report. Sign the letter with your full formal name and include:

- Your full name—printed.
- Your spouse's full name—if you have one.

- Your addresses for the last five years.
- Your social security number.
- Your date of birth.

If you have been declined credit by someone, you should enclose a copy of a letter that declined you. In that situation, TRW will not charge you for the report. Otherwise, the cost will range from about $15 to $25.

What will you receive? A report that includes eight kinds of information:

1. Personal identification data: your name, address and social security number.

2. The overall status of your credit accounts. For TRW reports, there's something called an "account profile" which has a positive column which shows where you've paid your accounts as agreed, a negative column which shows where you haven't, and a non-evaluated column which indicates that no evaluation of your credit has been given to the credit bureau by that particular account.

3. The names of all the companies who have extended credit to you. Examples might be Sears, banks, clothing stores such as Lord & Taylor, automobile finance companies, VISAs and MasterCards.

4. The types of accounts you have with each company. For example, you might have a line of credit with a bank, a charge account with a store, or a revolving credit arrangement with an appliance store.

5. Any delinquencies you have.

6. The terms of the credit. In other words, how large your debt is, how much you have left to pay, what you pay per month, and so forth.

7. A place where you have the right to make statements regarding your credit. For example, I once had a "delinquent" American Express bill. In my opinion, they had overbilled me and then labeled me delinquent before any payment was actually due. I submitted a statement to that effect to TRW to put into my credit record. By law, I had the right to have that statement appear right on my report. As another example, a November 1988 *Glamour* magazine article had a statement by a woman that she had purchased a television set using her VISA at an appliance store. The television never worked correctly. She "complained a lot" until the appliance store finally agreed to work out a deal with her. According to her statement, once the store gave her a satisfactory set she was willing to pay the debt.

Don't hesitate to make statements if you think there might be the slightest concern on the part of anyone reading your credit report. It shows that you understand the importance of good credit and are willing to take the time to set the record straight.

8. Whether any inquiries have been made to see your credit history—and who made them. TRW has a terrific brochure, "Understanding TRW's Credit Reporting Service," which might also be helpful to you. When you ask for your credit report, ask them to send a brochure along as well.

YOUR MONTHLY BUDGET

If you are a detail junkie, you will enjoy this next exercise. If you aren't, brace yourself. Like going to a dentist's office, monthly budgets are one of those have-to-do tasks faced by all entrepreneurs. Worse, it isn't something that you can ball park. At a minimum, you will need to make estimates of the following costs. Try to go to the dollar. Ask people who have run businesses to help. Ask your accountant to help. Ask your banker to help. And know that, when you are done, you will probably underestimate your costs by 20 percent to 40 percent because you're an optimist:

Types of Expenses	Monthly Costs	According to Whom? (in other words, where did you get the information?)
• Rent (Even if it's your house, you need to figure out how much of it you are using for tax purposes.)		
• Utilities —Lights —Heat (electric) —Heat (gas) —Water —Air conditioning		
• Telephone		
• FAX		
• Computer costs —Computer —Printer —Supplies —Software —Repair		
• Insurance —Building —Company —Rent —Workers' Compensation —Liability		

Types of Expenses	Monthly Costs	According to Whom? (in other words, where did you get the information?)
• Bank charges —Checking —Loan —Line of credit —VISA (yours) —VISA (customers')		
• Staff —Salaries —Benefits		
• Taxes —City —County —State —Federal		
• Car —Payment —Mileage (28 cents/mile)		
• Sales and Marketing Costs —Trade Shows —Brochures —Public Relations —Advertising —Market Research —Samples —Events		
• Stationery/Envelopes		
• Business Cards		
• Printer costs for customer gifts or promotional items		

Types of Expenses	Monthly Costs	According to Whom? (in other words, where did you get the information?)
• Coffee/tea and other beverage costs		
• Office food costs (birthday cakes, pizza)		
• Maintenance		
• Entertainment expenses —Gifts		
• Professional fees —Accountant —Attorney		
• Furniture costs		
• Plants (if you must)		

If you manufacture a product, you also need to figure out all the costs of supplies for your product, and you may need to add the costs of an additional space (that is, where you'll be making your products) and machinery-related expenses.

Once you think you've figured out your expenses, show them to as many people as you think will take the time to review them to see if they can come up with anything else. When you feel that you are as close as you can come, add a last line to your expenses: contingency expenses—and make that 20 percent of the total cost of everything else. There will be something you haven't thought of. This is one of those truths. If I'm wrong (I won't be), you can write me a letter thanking me for helping you to stash that money for the five-day spa vacation you've been wanting to take for years.

BOOKKEEPING SYSTEMS

No company can survive without a bookkeeping system. And life has become too complicated for shoe boxes to work anymore. When the accountants with whom I work make speeches about basic bookkeeping systems, they tell entrepreneurs that you need an eight-part system. If you are planning simply to hire a bookkeeper—something I urge you to do—skip this section and move on to cash flow. If you insist on doing the bookkeeping yourself, let me just say that I think you are making a mistake and that there are more productive ways to use your time. Now that I've said it, here's the system. You need:

- A corporate business checking account. Remember, keep your personal and business accounts separate or you and your accountant will regret it. And the IRS won't treat you kindly if they ever decide to audit the company. Also remember to reconcile the account monthly.

- A way to record expenses. A chart of accounts is your starting point. It is what it sounds like—a listing of your accounts. A cash disbursements journal. There are software packages that can do this for you. A lot of my clients use Peachtree or Real World. I have no idea how good they are. A computer hack/accountant type can tell you. A filing system to track invoices. You'll have two types: unpaid invoices—file them in an "open invoice" file by payment date so you can track them—and paid invoices. Mark invoices paid with the date and your check number as soon as you've paid them. I then file them by vendor in alphabetical files.

- A way to record sales and cash receipts. A chart of accounts is your starting point here, too. Start with a sales journal, which records sales. Again, there are lots of software packages that can do this. You also need a cash receipts journal to track when people have paid you. Yes, software can help here, too. If your cash receipts are going to be used to record sales, the cash receipts subject to sales tax should be separated from nontaxable items to save you time later.

- A general ledger. Use this to prepare monthly financial statements.

- If you have any assets (that is, money or things you could sell for money), you'll want to set up a fixed asset journal. It should list: all your assets; the date each asset was purchased and the date you started using it if different from purchase date; a description of each asset; its cost; depreciation method and life (get your accountant to help you on this); the date you sold it if you don't have it anymore.

- A petty-cash journal. Petty cash gets everyone in trouble. It's a pain in the neck to track. On the other hand, if you don't track it, you could find yourself losing a lot of money over the long haul. Change and dollars always have a unique way of slipping through entrepreneurs' fingers without leaving clues. Keep an ongoing petty cash balance sheet (that is, when you put money into the petty cash account, and how much, and when you've taken it out). I like to use prenumbered slips to issue petty cash and attach a slip to say what it was used for. A check should be written from the general checking account to reimburse petty cash. Never use personal money for this. It becomes an accountant's nightmare.

- If you have inventory, you need inventory records. It's also important to take physical inventory periodically, say monthly or quarterly, to see what you really have.

- If you have employees, you'll also need payroll records. You'll need personnel files maintained for each staff person. At a minimum, the following information should be included: federal and state and other withholding authorizations (the W-4 forms you've signed all these years); documentation of their pay rate or salary; their social security numbers. Then a payroll journal can be prepared for each person: the employee name (and employee number if used); hours worked and hourly rate or gross salary as applicable; withholding; net pay and payroll check number. Individual payroll records for each employee need to contain their cumulative gross wages to date (this is updated everytime someone is paid) and their cumulative withholding amounts to date (federal, state, and city, FICA—social security, other).

Each of these components needs to be tracked on a regular basis, with a hard-core look at the end of every month.

As I said, the easiest (and in the end cheapest) route is to find someone else to get you started—either by helping you to set up the system or by doing your bookkeeping for you.

CASH FLOW

I've discovered that most women understand the individual journals. What does us in is putting all the financial information together so we have some way of knowing whether we're making money or losing it. You'd be amazed at how often people think they are making money hand over foot when really they are hemorrhaging cash. Hi-tech companies and service companies are notorious for this. I remember a local software company that lost a dollar every time they sold a unit of software. Their response: to sell a whole lot more software. Wrong.

You need to understand your cash flow so you know what to do and when to do it. If what I'm about to write doesn't explain it sufficiently, you'll need to find someone who does understand your cash flow and is willing to go over it again and again until it clicks. (It's a lot like learning to play music. If you just keep going over it, sooner or later it starts to make sense. Honest.) I would try to find another woman to teach you, because we speak the same language, tend to learn in the same manner, and are from the same planet.

If you don't have cash, you won't survive. It doesn't matter how gorgeous your building is. Or that you've just received the Woman Entrepreneur of the Year award. If you don't have cash coming in to pay your bills, your business won't last. Period.

There is only one way to track the health of your company and that is to watch your cash flow. Understanding how cash moves through your business helps you to do this. (This is a good time to go get some chocolate or caffeine or to do whatever makes your head clear and your thinking sharp.) Allright, here goes.

First the cash flow picture:

CASH

INCREASES THROUGH:	DECREASES THROUGH:
Accounts receivable	Accounts payable
Sales	Production costs
	Operations costs
	Inventory

From the day of your first sale you will have a cycle of money coming in and going out. It goes out when you buy materials and services and when you pay people what you owe them. It comes in when your customers pay you. This may not be the same as when they buy from you. Think of your VISA card. You may buy a dress today with it, but you won't actually pay for it until you get your VISA bill, and maybe not even then if you're like me.

The money that you have to work with at any one time is known in the accounting world as *net working capital*. You need to know this term (partly because people won't expect you to—it's an easy way to surprise banking industry types with your brilliance). Here's what your net working capital is. Let's say you have some cash on hand and you have some assets that can be turned into cash pretty quickly. For most women, these assets are simply the money our customers owe us. You might also have supplies or inventory (parts of your products) that you could sell if you had to.

At the same time, you will also owe people money that you need to pay within the next year so your suppliers don't come to break your knuckles. These are "liabilities." You might also owe the bank loan payments, have rent payments, staff salaries, and business-related VISA bills.

Figuring out the shape you are in is easy. You simply add up all your cash and things you could quickly "sell" for cash—those are your current assets. Then you add up all bills and payments you need to pay off prontito—those are your current liabilities. Now. Subtract your liabilities from your assets. If there is a zero balance or some money left over, you're okay for now. If the number is negative, you need to figure out what you're going to do to find money to pay your bills.

How do you turn this exercise into a "flow"? Brace your-self. You need to understand this, so keep reading this section over until it makes sense. Not understanding it is equivalent to running your business on faith. Unlike faith, hard work and a clear understanding of what's going on is the real key to success.

The Small Business Administration booklet "Understanding Cash Flow" does the best job I've seen of explaining flow, so I'll quote directly from them (because I don't like this stuff any more than you do).

> One way to measure the flow of cash and the firm's ability to maintain its cash or liquid assets is to compute *working capital*. It is the difference between current assets and current liabilities. The change in this value from period to period [say month to month] is called *net working capital*. For example:

	Month 20 19×1	Month 21 19×2
Current Assets	$110,000	$200,000
Less Current Liabilities	–70,000	–112,000
Working Capital	40,000	88,000
Net Working Capital Increase (Decrease)		$48,000

> Net working capital increased during the [month], but we don't know how. It could have been all in cash or all in inventory. Or, it may have resulted from a reduction in accounts payable.

> *Cash Flow Statement.* While net working capital shows only the changes in the current position, a "flow" statement explains the changes that have occurred in any account during any time period. The change in the cash account can be readily determined if you know net working capital and the changes in current liabilities and current assets other than cash.

> Let:
> NWC   be net working capital
> CA   be the change in current assets other than cash

CL   be the change in current liabilities

cash   be the change in cash

Because net working capital is the difference between the change in current assets and current liabilities,

NWC = CA + cash − CL

cash   = NWC − CA + CL

This relationship states that if we know net working capital (NWC), the change in current liabilities (CL), and the change in current assets less cash (CA less cash), we can calculate the change in cash. The change in cash is then added to the beginning balance of cash to determine the ending balance.

Suppose you forecast that sales will increase $50,000 and the following will correspondingly change:

Receivables	increase by $25,000
Inventory	increase by $70,000
Accounts Payable	increase by $30,000
Notes Payable	increase by $10,000

Using net working capital of $48,000, what is the projected change in cash?

cash   = NWC − CA + CL

        = 48,000 − 25,000 − 70,000 + 30,000 + 10,000

        = −7,000

Conclusion: Over this time period, under the condition of increasing sales volume, cash decreased by $7,000. Is there enough cash to cover this decrease? This will depend upon the beginning cash balance.

Here's a chart I share with my clients to help them better to understand the flow of money through the business.

CASH FLOW FOR 199_

	Jan	Feb	Mar	Apr	May	Jun	Jul	Aug	Sep	Oct	Nov	Dec
Your receipts (you get these): Cash sales Collection or Receivables Other sources												
Total (A)												
Payments (you pay these): Cash purchases Payments on accounts Wages and Salaries Other payments												
Expenses: Rent Insurance Light, Heat, Power Repairs and Maintenance Leasing Bank charges and interest Telephone and Postage Advertising Public Relations Memberships Entertainment Other payments												
Other items you have to pay: Purchase of Fixed Assets (such as a computer) Tax payments Fees to accountant Fees to attorney Loan repayments Other payments												
Total (B)												
Net Inflow (A-B)/Outflow (B-A)												
Balance brought forward from previous month												
Balance for this month												

Try filling out the chart on your own. If you still can't figure it out, get your accountant to explain it. If she can't help you to understand it, find a new accountant. This is only the first of many times when you'll need someone to talk you through financial information. So do it right. Just wait until you decide to take the company public!

BALANCE SHEETS

My bias is that cash-flow statements are the only real financial information you need to understand to build your business. Unfortunately for both of us, the rest of the world insists on balance sheets as a source of information about a company as well. Now some people, who end up being accountants, spend years perfecting their understanding of balance sheets. And if you are an accountant, you will cringe at how simplified I'm about to sound. The truth is, companies owned by women rarely use balance sheets—at least historically. Since most of our businesses are services, we usually don't own a lot of stuff. Not like manufacturers. Balance sheets were created for manufacturing firms.

Having said all this, you still need to know what a balance sheet is and be able to put one together with the help of your bookkeeper or accountant, so you'll have one for the bank if they want one.

Three kinds of information are summarized on your balance sheet: assets, liabilities and equity. Your assets are money or money equivalents (that is, things you could sell for money if you had to). There are two types of assets: current and fixed. Current assets are cash and things you can turn into cash within a short time period—say a year. So you would include money your customers owe you (accounts receivable), inventory you can sell within a year, and the like. Fixed assets or long-term assets are things that might take longer to turn into cash. The normal categories are buildings, equipment such as computers, machinery, company cars, and so forth.

Liabilities are what you owe. Current liabilities are the things you have to pay within a year. Included would be payments to your suppliers, bank loan payments, staff expenses, and so forth. Long-term liabilities might include loan payments to your investors, a mortgage on your building, and so forth.

What a balance sheet does is allow you to add up the value of all your assets and then add up the value of all your liabilities. Your goal is to have assets that are worth more than your liabilities, because that means you have more cash potentially available to you than the bills and loans you have to pay out. If you subtract the sum of your liabilities from the sum of your assets and have anything left over, that leftover amount is called "equity," or retained earnings.

I've never quite understood equity—it's not something you can touch, taste, smell, see, or dance with. On the other hand, bankers love it because it tells them you have a healthy company, and if your retained earnings increase every year it should mean you have more money in the bank or at least you have a company that is accumulating value so you can sell it for a good price when you're ready.

Chart E is the most simple balance sheet you'll find anywhere today. Take it to your accountant and have her massage it for you until it better reflects you and the company you are creating.

CHART E
BALANCE SHEET

ASSETS	When you open the business	End Year 1	End Year 2	End Year 3
Current Assets: Cash Accounts Receivable Inventories Other				
Total Current Assets				
Fixed Assets: Building Equipment Furniture and fixtures Company car				
Total Assets				
LIABILITIES				
Current Liabilities: Accounts Payable Note Payable Note Payable - Other Trade Notes Payable Payroll and Withholding Taxes				
Total Current Liabilities				
Long-term Liabilities: Note Payable—Bank Miscellaneous Note Payable				
Total Liabilities				

	When you open the business	End Year 1	End Year 2	End Year 3
Equity: Retained Earnings				
Total Equity				
Total Liabilities and Equity				

STAYING OUT OF JAIL

Money is important to everyone. Especially the government. You need to keep careful, detailed track of the money associated with your business. You need to know where every penny comes from and where every penny goes. That's why you need to understand your cash flow—so you know what is going on for real.

You can't be casual about this. Here are some other things that, over the years, have gotten companies into serious trouble with the government. Avoid them. You don't want to spar with the Internal Revenue Service. They always win.

Here are your nevers:

NEVER:

- Forget to list and set aside all the taxes you need to pay as you accumulate them. This includes sales, state, city, federal, payroll and workers' compensation payments.
- Borrow from your tax account to pay other bills.

- Mix personal expenses with business expenses. You'll rue the day you did.
- Barter without figuring out the value of what you bartered. In the eyes of the government, bartering is equivalent to your selling something (whatever you bartered with) and buying something (whatever you bartered for).

Enough of this financial hoopla. Take a break before you go on to Chapter 5. You deserve it.

MORE MONEY ISSUES:

FINDING FINANCING

You will need to raise money for your company. Everyone does. Don't take it personally. You just will. This one is rough for women. For years I've watched women sabotaging themselves when they raise money by not doing the homework I know they can do before applying for a loan, or by waiting too long before looking, or by raising only a portion of what they need when there is no way a business can be built on such a paltry sum.

Why? I think we don't want to owe. I think that in the back of our minds we have this belief that if we owe a man or men (and they're still the ones with the money), they'll expect at least partial payment in the form of sexual favors. In our minds, we'll become their indentured servants—or worse.

Men ask for money. They ask all the time. They ask for a lot. They don't hesitate. Even a little. They perceive themselves as excellent investments for anyone who takes the slightest interest in their companies. We need to do more of that. We need to see ourselves as opportunities—and our companies as worthy and smart investments. We need to remember that owing someone money is just that, owing them money.

So, why will you need money? There are five reasons:

1. Things never go the way you think they will. Even with anally-compulsive planning you may need to throw away your logo, letterhead, and start over. Or redo your tax records. Every time things don't go the way you planned, the cost is in money.

2. Everything will cost twice as much as you think. You'll look at your brochure and decide it needs a third color and an additional panel. You'll find the perfect office space and it just happens to be in the most expensive building in the city. You'll find the perfect receptionist and his last job was as executive secretary to a partner in an international accounting firm. He wants to work for you, but can't keep his lifestyle at the $5.25 an hour you had hoped to offer.

3. Things take twice as long to get done as you think they will. And time is money. If you have to wait twice as long as you planned for your computer to be hooked up, then your proposal to a client will take twice as long to get out and you'll need money to feed yourself while you wait.

4. If you are just starting a business, you will probably need to go on faith for your first year to year and a half before the business really kicks in. You'll need money to buy food.

5. Ironically, growth creates a need for financing. Women business owners are always asking, "How can I tell when I need money to grow?" Fortunately, there are clear signs. When you get to a point where some part of you is saying, "I think I need more money to keep going here," it's time to review the following checklist. If you check only one or two, you can probably keep going without an input of capital. If you check more, it's time to find some money to help you grow. I first heard this checklist from John Psarouthakis, then president of J. P. Industries. He has since written a book on growing your company, *Managing the Growing Firm*, which I highly recommend.

- ☐ You don't have time to prepare for unexpected calamities.
- ☐ Your resources are spread too thinly.
- ☐ There is this insatiable need for inventory, space, equipment, more people.
- ☐ Your day-to-day activities are greatly speeding up.
- ☐ There are never enough hours in your day.
- ☐ You spend too much time putting out fires. Every time you turn around there is a new crisis.
- ☐ If you have staff, they aren't aware of each other and what they are doing.
- ☐ You are desperate for a good manager.
- ☐ You increasingly feel as if you are the only one who can get things done correctly.
- ☐ Increasingly, things just don't get done.
- ☐ Your sales are growing, but you aren't making any money.

THE PROCESS

STAGE I

The process of raising money resembles the search for the perfect mate. There are clear stages, just as in dating. First, you need to get yourself in order. But, instead of a new hair color (the politically correct color is now dark brown—have you noticed?) and ten less pounds, you need to:

- Make sure your credit report is clean. If you last checked it six months ago, check it again.
- Write your business plan (more on that in Chapter 6).
- Set up a bookkeeping system that will work for you.

- Have an accountant.
- Have an attorney.
- Have a bank and a business account, however small.
- Have business cards you can leave behind.
- Have a letterhead (which means you also need a company name, address, and telephone number to put on that letterhead) so you can thank people as you meet them.
- Have two incredibly expensive-looking business suits. (I buy mine at second-hand stores. I've found that very wealthy women have short attention spans when it comes to business suits. They seem to wear them only once or twice. At the same time, they have wonderful taste. So, I let them "choose" my suits for me and wear them a few times to break them in. As a result, I have to pay only $100 to $150 for the suit instead of $500 to $600 when it's my turn to own it.) You need two of these, because you don't want to wear the same suit to a follow-up meeting with investors.
- Have an elegant pair of expensive earrings and a good watch. (I have one asset, a Rolex watch. It's amazing how effective it is when I'm meeting with investors—I always make sure to check the time frequently in a meeting until they notice. Why? Because when they notice the watch, they perceive me as successful, which means that I must know what I'm talking about, right?!)

When you have yourself in order, you are ready to dance.

STAGE II

The first part of stage two is to know exactly what you are after. Like mating, if you don't know what you want, you won't get it.

Ask yourself these questions:

1. How much money do I need? Remember, your cash-flow analysis will tell you how much you need and when you need it. Double that amount, because things will go wrong and finding financing will take you twice as long as you planned, which means you'll be subsidizing the business for a while longer.

2. What stage of growth am I in? There are basically three stages of growth where companies need money. In the first stage, you

   - are proving your product concept. In other words, you might have prototypes out there or be doing customer surveys to find out what people want.
   - are doing everything yourself.

In the second stage of growth, most companies

- have their products completed and in place.
- have initiated marketing (that is, have started selling the product).
- have established their manufacturing capabilities if they are producing a product themselves.
- have hired some staff.
- are thinking about the next generation of products they will be selling.

In stage three, most companies have had some sales, but they need money to expand their marketing efforts, to hire more management (and machinery if they are building products) and to put systems in place that will help manage the growth.

What stage are you in? _____

The other questions you need to answer are:

1. What is your geographical market? _____

_____

2. What industry are you in? _____

_____

The point of these questions is that you do not want to waste your time talking to a potential investor if he or she doesn't understand your industry. By the same token, you do not want to find someone who is too far away, because he or she won't be interested. Something like 90 percent of all investors make investments in companies that are within a sixty-minute drive from their office. And you don't want to talk to risk-adverse people if you are in your first stage of growth. You want risk takers. Gamblers. Probably other entrepreneurs who have made money on their own companies and are sniffing around for something to sink some money into. Profile yourself so you can screen out wasted meetings with the wrong people. Think of this as trying to date a Republican when you grew up in a family of die-hard Democrats—a real relationship is just too long a shot. By the time you are in your second stage, you will probably be able to access more conservative people like your father and possibly a banker.

Where are these financial resources? They are everywhere. Once you've profiled yourself, you can start telling everyone you know what you're looking for and who you think fits the bill. Over the years, I've learned that persistence is everything when it comes to looking for money. I know a fellow who was turned down by 147 investors before he raised the money he needed to start his business. My rule of thumb is that you need to talk to everyone you know and ask these people to talk to the people they know and ask those people to talk to their friends. Am I starting to remind you of the game of "telephone" we all played as kids? Now, be careful not to formally offer to sell shares of your company to anyone for an investment until you've screened them the way they'll screen you. You'll also run into Securities and Exchange Commission Regulations (yes, even you), so have your attorney look over your shoulder during the process of finding investors.

A useful exercise is to put yourself in the place of potential investors and ask yourself what would they want to see from you. The first thing is strength. This is no time to be wimpy or demure. You need to be forthright about your vision for where you are headed and why you will succeed. You want to act as though you are doing them a favor by talking to them. I don't mean to be arrogant. The role is more one of a gracious hostess where you are delighted that they've found you and have this wonderful opportunity to make themselves some money. *Remember this:* We women tend to come across as needy when we are raising money—even though we aren't. Maybe it's because we don't shout out the amount we're after. Maybe it's because I still can't get my clients to stop looking down when they name the amount. Don't sabotage yourself. Please. Look your potential investors in the eye and be ready to rattle off three to five reasons why you are an excellent investment and watch how well people respond. Even if they don't invest, they will be more apt to refer you to someone else who might be interested.

No matter who the investors are—whether they're bankers, venture capitalists, friends, suppliers—they will look for at least these things:

- That you have a proven track record as a manager.
- That you *know* the industry you are in.
- That you have committed a substantial proportion of your personal resources to the venture. (Don't worry about this one. By the time you track these folks down, you will have put all kinds of time, money, and other resources in the business.)

- That you understand marketing and have a strong marketing orientation (and that you can somehow prove that you do).

- That you have an "unfair advantage." In other words, that there is something singularly special about you or your product. As venture capitalists like to describe it, you are the equivalent of a violin repairer who goes to heaven. Everybody wants your product. A friend of mine has developed disposable paper bikini underpants for women that can be used for all kinds of emergencies. They are attractive, sturdy, comfortable, and biodegradable. You know yourself how long women have been waiting for these! She had investors approaching her before she even knew how much money she needed to raise. If only she would work on no-run panty hose. Then we'd all be set.

- That you have a plan for growth and that it's rational.

- That your plan for growth allows for paying back their investment.

- That you have a product that has fairly high margins. In other words, you can expect a solid profit every time you sell a unit. What does this mean for you? One thing is that it is difficult to raise money for retail stores, because the margins tend to be quite low. The same is true for food products. Margins in most grocery stores are under 1 percent, which means that one mistake can put you into a losing spin.

- That the market you are selling to is large and growing. In other words, they will want to know that you will always have customers and that there will be more and more of those customers.

- That you don't have too much competition. Everyone has some competitors. Investors become very nervous when they see more than three or four key players in a market. The reason is that as the competition heats up, price wars often begin. And when that happens, the youngest and smallest companies die first.

WHAT TO LOOK FOR IN A BANK

Trying to find a good small-business bank? The truth is, despite what bank advertisements say, many banks aren't interested in small companies. Since there are some 14,000 banks in the United States, we can't tell you which banks are best in Tampa, or Topeka, or wherever it is your company is located. But, based on what business owners have told us, here are some of the bank and banker qualities we think are worth searching for.

Banking knowledge. Few bankers will intentionally lead you astray. But, Dan Lang, co-owner of Nature's Warehouse, a $6 million baked goods business in Sacramento, recently discovered that some bankers have a tighter grip than others on what's possible in a given situation. Lang and his partner recently met with lending officers at several banks to try to get $1 million in financing to help buy Nature's Warehouse. But, only one—the lending officer at Sacramento Commercial Bank—"said right away he could do it as a 10-year SBA loan. Without hesitating, he knew what he could and couldn't do."

Sense of urgency. "Banker's hours," may be a fading notion, but a CEO's idea of a "quick turnaround" and a banker's are often days, even weeks, apart. Tom Kinder, co-owner of Pure Podunk, a bedding products mail-order business in Sharon, Vermont, found that his bankers at Vermont National Bank were able—and extremely willing—to meet his compressed timetable for a recent $100,000 loan. Kinder says he got calls even during evenings at home, updating him on the progress.

continued

Teaching talent. Many bankers can't—or don't want to—articulate what they expect from customers and how the bank makes its decisions. But, Dwight Mulch, president of three-year-old Preferred Products Corp., a building materials distributor in Burlington, Iowa, says he gets both types of information from his lending officer at First Start Bank and has benefited greatly. "When I was starting," says Mulch, "he practically led me around by the nose. He showed me what to put in the plan, and he still tells me how the system works."

Industry knowledge. Whatever industry you're in, it helps to have a banker who has had some exposure to your type of business, says Dave Sanger, president of Resource Solution Group, a computer-consulting business in Southfield, Michigan. Sanger's lending officer at Manufacturers Bank in Detroit, "knows we don't have the same kind of assets as a retailer or a manufacturer," Sanger says, "and she knows the terminology."

Financial Stability. Given a choice, Kevin Whalen, chief financial officer of Twin Modal Inc., a Minneapolis transportation brokerage firm, didn't pick the bank that was offering the most aggressive deal. And it's a good thing, too, he says: "That bank has had real problems with the regulators and has pulled way back." Before selecting Marquette Bank, in 1989, Whalen, a former banker himself, did spreadsheet comparisons of several banks, comparing returns on assets, capital-to-asset ratios, and so on. "I felt that, in the long run, we'd be better off with the most conservative bank around."

Managers with backbone. Banks have policies, notes Mike Walker, president of Walker Communications Inc., a public-relations firm in Scottsdale, Arizona. "But you want to have a manager with the courage to override them if it makes sense to do so." Walker's branch manager at First Interstate Bank of Arizona, for instance, allows him to draw on checks immediately after they're deposited and often acts as a troubleshooter for him within the bank. "I don't know what the manual says," offers Walker, "but you need somebody who can take a stand."

A LOAN CHECKLIST

Before you go to see your banker, decide for yourself what you really want. This checklist will help you to prepare:

- Type of loan wanted (line of credit, revolving, etc.)
- Amount
- Use of proceeds
- Length of time you want the loan
- Date you want to close
- How much money you'll need at closing
- Collateral you can offer
- Rate you expect
- Your proposed repayment schedule
- Any co-signers or other guarantees you have up your sleeve
- Where the money will come from for repayment
- Other sources of funds for repayment if your first idea doesn't work

THE DEAL-MAKING DANCE

Once you've found somebody interested in investing in you, the real courtship begins. It also has stages that often take longer than one would expect. The fastest I've ever seen anyone locate financing was three months; most entrepreneurs will need six months to a year, so you can't start too soon.

The first stage of the deal making dance is where you first meet, circle each other, and decide whether you like each other. (If you don't like [and trust] your potential investor, keep looking. If one person is seriously interested in you, there will be others. Honest.) In this first stage, you give the investor your business plan, define the amount of financing needed, and how it will be used. The investor usually makes a ball-park guess about what he thinks the value of the company will be when it's all grown-up. The valuation is what gives him his first clue regarding his potential return on investment, or how much money he could really make on the deal.

In the second stage, the investor does his due diligence. Put another way, he takes a harder and closer look at you. He'll call all the references he'll have asked you for. He'll ask to see all the legal documentation you have regarding your business so far. If he's really good, he'll do his own market research to see if he comes up with the same customers that you believe you'll get. He'll ask other people about competition. If you have a technology-based product, he may pay someone to do an independent technology assessment to see where you fit in the industry. And he may do all these things several times over. I have one associate who had venture capitalists check more than forty references before they invested in him. When I asked the investors why, they said they just kept going until they heard some bad news—they knew that everyone has weaknesses and just wanted to *identify* his before they continued the negotiations. Another investor friend of mine told me that he always has at least three long visits with entrepreneurs as a part of his due diligence. The first time he has people come to him at his office. There he spends most of the time describing himself, his history, and his value set to make certain that the entrepreneur is honestly interested in working with him. Then he goes to spend a day with the entrepreneur in her environment, watching how she organizes tasks, how she spends her time, and how she deals with other people. During that meeting, he asks many, many questions. One of his goals is to discover situations that put the entrepreneur under a great deal of stress. The third meeting is that stressful situation. Put another way, if she hates sailing, he takes her sailing. Afraid of heights? They go mountain climbing. A lousy golfer? They golf. The point is to see the entrepreneur under a great deal of stress so he can watch how she deals with it. Is she calm? Honest? Organized? Does she simply accept the situation and deal with it as best she can? He's learned that much of an entrepreneur's life is stress-filled (have you noticed?), and how you deal with stress is key to your success.

Once you pass the due diligence test (and you will now that you know the rules), the last phase of financing is the actual negotiation of the deal. This is where investors tell you how much they are willing to invest and what terms they want. Do they want this to be a loan, where you simply pay them back their money and some interest (like your VISA cards)? What interest rate do they want? Or do they want a percentage of ownership in the company in return for their investment and, if they do, what is the percentage? Do they want any special security from you, such as a loan on your house? Don't deal without help. First decide what kind of a deal is acceptable to you so you'll know when to say no thank you and walk away (let me remind you again that if you've found one investor you'll find others). Use an attorney to review any and all documents.

What kind of money is out there? There are basically two kinds of money for your company—loans and equity investments. The best way to think about this is to study the following chart. Basically, all investors can be characterized by how they relate to risk and what kind of a return on investment they want for their money. If you are a "low-risk" deal (either you don't need the money really, you have a co-signer who has the money but would rather you got it somewhere else, or you have enough collateral to pay for the loan if the company can't pay it back), then bankers are your target. They'll give you loans at *low interest*, relative to everyone else. If, on the other hand, you don't have what you need to cover a loan if you go bust, then you are considered to be a riskier deal. In this case, you probably won't be able to get bank financing and will have to go to equity investors for help. They will charge you higher interest rates, and they will probably expect some ownership in the company:

Your goal is to be as low a risk as possible. So, if you can self-finance yourself until you have sales, so much the better. If you can get purchase orders before you go to investors, that is good. If you can back your financing with personal assets, you'll end up in a better negotiating position. Get as much as you can in the form of loans and sell equity only when you absolutely have to.

YES, THERE IS A SIMPLE WAY

Since almost all women actually start their businesses with less than $50,000, I'm going to tell you the process I used to get a line of credit worth $50,000. (A line of credit is the same thing as a loan, except you don't have to pay interest on anything until you actually use the money.) The trick here is time. The process took me a year. I started out by going to my friendly neighborhood credit union (of which I was a member) and telling their loan officer that I wanted to establish a line of credit. She said that was fine as long as I had a reason, so I figured I'd ask for enough to buy a mink coat (these were the days when mink coats were politically correct). Since I was a member of the credit union and had about $500 in a savings account, she gave me a line of credit for $2,000, using my savings account and my car as collateral. I used the $2,000 and paid it back and went back for more. Now, the point here is that *I didn't use my own money.* I used my money to leverage someone else's. That's what you want to do. As much as you can. The second time I got $5,000 for a car, which I borrowed and paid back. By the third time, all I had to do was call the credit union and ask them to increase my line of credit to $10,000. I just kept repeating this until I had all the money I needed. Which they did. Now whenever I go to a new city, I go through the same process on principle—you just never know when you'll need $50,000.

Once you find your banker, ask her what you need to do to start a similar process. A good banker will urge you to get started and tell you exactly what to do.

WHAT BANKERS LIKE

Let's say you don't have several years to play the credit-line advance game. I would still see if I could position myself for a loan from a banker. I would set up a formal meeting and take my business plan with me. Be prepared to answer the following questions:

1. What is your background? (Here the banker is looking for a description of the company and the owner.)
2. Why do you need the loan?
3. How much money do you need?
4. When will you need it?
5. What will it be used for?
6. When can the funds be repaid? (Refer to your cash flow projections to show her.)
7. How will the loan be repaid? From the collection of receivables, sale of inventory, sale of fixed assets, profits?
8. What will you use for collateral (in case those things don't do it)?
9. What is your contingency plan if the company doesn't go as planned? (Don't worry about this now. You'll figure out contingencies as part of the business plan described in the next chapter.)

While you are answering these questions, the banker will be looking for what they fondly refer to as the five C's of lending:

1. Your character (whether she trusts you).
2. Your capacity or ability to pay back the loan.
3. The capital or money that is already in the company (that is, any assets you could sell if you had to).
4. The condition of the economy generally and your industry in particular (that is, whether the outside world will support your efforts).
5. The collateral you have to back the loan (bank accounts, your house, car, machinery, stock, and so forth).

Although most banks have their own loan applications, the following chart offers a generic example of the kind of information you'll be asked to provide:

PERSONAL FINANCIAL STATEMENT
As of _____, 19__

Name   Residence Phone

Residence Address

City, State & Zip

Business Name

ASSETS		LIABILITIES	
Cash on hand and in banks	$_____	Accounts payable	$_____
Savings accounts	_____	Notes payable	_____
IRAs	_____	Installment accounts (auto)	_____
Accounts and notes receivable	_____	Monthly payments	$_____
Life insurance—cash	_____	Installment accounts (other)	_____
Stocks and bonds	_____	Monthly payments	$_____
Real estate	_____	Loans on life insurance	_____
Automobile—present value	_____	Mortgages on real estate	_____
Other personal property	_____	Unpaid taxes	_____
Other assets	_____	Other liabilities	_____
		Total liabilities	_____
		Net worth	_____
TOTAL	$_____	TOTAL	$_____

Section 1. Source of Income		Contingent Liabilities	
Salary	$_____	As endorser or co-maker	$_____
Net investment income	_____	Legal claims and judgments	_____
Real estate income	_____	Provision for federal income tax	_____
Other income (alimony ex)	_____	Other special debt	_____

Section 2. Notes Payable to Banks and Others   +

Name and Address of Noteholder	Original Balance	Current Balance	Payment Amount	Terms (Monthly, etc.)	How Secured or Endorsed Type of Collateral

All your information will need to be backed up by documentation, and you'll probably have to bring in several years of personal tax returns.

Most bankers can turn a loan application around in a week and can tell you in an initial interview whether it's even worth applying. Even if you are turned down, ask the banker what you need to do to come back and get a loan and state your intention to follow that advice. Don't hesitate to ask if there are any government loan programs worth pursuing. The banker will know. Be sure to ask about a Small Business Administration loan—the banker will tell you if you are eligible and how to go about applying. Your state probably has at least one program you can access. And more and more cities and counties have some form of loan pool. Check them out. If you can't get a loan from these sources, then you can go after equity investors. You already know how to find them. Just keep persisting until you find a match.

CREATIVE FINANCING AS A LAST RESORT

Allright. You've memorized my advice, been macha woman for a year, and still no luck. Are there creative ways to finance your business? You bet. And they can be as creative as your imagination will allow. The two owners of A Woman's Prerogative, a bookstore in the Detroit area, presold gift certificates to raise their last $15,000. Your suppliers can help either by directly investing in you or by allowing you to slow pay on their bills. Customers will prepay if you have a product they really want. Employees may have money to invest. There are a lot of middle managers out there who have been un-golden-handcuffed and have $50,000 to $100,000 in their pockets. They don't want to necessarily start a company, but may be willing to invest in the firm that has the job they want. I see this more and more. My brother started a construction company on VISA cards. I have a friend who built apartment buildings in Chicago on VISA-card credit. At his height, I think he had about forty cards. (I don't think you can do that anymore—it's the idea that counts.) Don't be afraid to barter: You can trade for printing, space, staff, food, supplies, child care, transportation, just about anything. Just keep the details for when you do your tax returns, because bartering is treated as a business transaction. There are companies who finance purchase orders. There are companies who will buy your car, computer, machinery, and maybe even furniture from you and lease it back to you. There might be a joint-venture partner out there in the form of a company who has a self-interest in your success. I've seen manufacturer representatives get financing from the companies they are repping for, as an example.

If you have real grit, you might want to acquire another company that has assets that you can then use to collateralize a loan. The possibilities are endless. Just stay legal. No mafia money. No drug money. No cash from suitcases.

BOTTOM-LINE STREET SMARTS

Some last words on financing—or lessons I've learned the hard way:

- Don't jump for your first offer. Like your first job, the offer may not be the best you'll get. Wait to see what else comes in.
- Piece your sources of financing together—go for as much debt as you can get, because the bank is the cheapest money, and then go for equity.
- Look under rocks. Money can be found in pretty strange places. Don't overlook grants, or federal sources, or sub-contracts with larger firms.
- Don't give away the baby with the bath. Hang on to as much control as possible as long as you can. Never sell more than 50 percent ownership unless you are certain that is your *only* option.
- The process will take twice as long as you think. Give yourself time.
- Don't assume family members are your best investors. If they invest and look over your shoulder daily, the way most family members do, it will make you crazy. You need good *businesswomen* on your side—not mothers (unless they've owned a business, of course).

CHAPTER 6

THE BUSINESS PLAN

THE MOTHER OF ALL DOCUMENTS

Trying to build a business without writing a business plan is like marrying someone when you've only seen his picture—you have the vision but you haven't figured out the details to make it work.

Dr. Geri Larkin

I remember the day when I first realized that men and women think very differently about business plans. I had an appointment with a woman who had been successfully manufacturing a retail product in her basement, earning more than $150,000 every year. She had just received a huge order for her product from one of the big chain retailers and needed some money for supplies. She decided to approach a bank for financing only to be told that she needed a business plan before she could be considered for a loan or line of credit.

When she showed up at my office for "Business Plans 101" I started to describe a plan the way I do to all my male clients only to watch her eyes glaze over with what felt like a combination of math fear, disbelief, and total frustration.

So I took a different tack. "Think of a business plan as a journal that looks forward instead of backward. Think of it as a method of planning that allows you to fast-forward how you want to develop your business." It worked. She relaxed. The process

101

The process became more female-friendly. We were both relieved and managed to hash out a plan within a week. (We could have done it in less time but we tried to write it without chocolate or caffeine at our fingertips. To this day I can't decide if it was a mistake to go without the chocolate.) She got the money.

You need a business plan. If the company is just you, you need a plan. If it's you and a partner you need a plan. If you have been in business for awhile you need a plan just as much as a burgeoning entrepreneur because the world is shifting in all kinds of directions and a plan will help you to assess the impact of those shifts on your business.

So what is a business plan? In the end, it's a strategy document. A plan defines who your company is, *what business* you are in (defining this is not as easy as it sounds), the goals you have for your company, and how you plan to achieve those goals. It's a valuable dry run because it forces you (and it's the only thing that does!) to take an objective, critical, and, I hope, unemotional look at your possible future.

Better than anything else you do, a good business plan can sell your vision for your company to two audiences that you need on your side to succeed. The first is your internal audiences. *You* are the first member of that audience. Almost every woman with whom I have ever written a business plan has remarked on how much less anxiety she felt once she wrote the plan. It helps you to relax. Think of it as preventative medicine. In my experience up to 40 percent of women who write business plans end up significantly changing their business or idea as they write. Some shift to different product lines. Others decide to expand their businesses in ways they never would have predicted without a plan. Some decide not to start a business because writing the plan is the first forewarning that running a business is tougher than their imaginations projected.

The second type of person who makes up your internal audience is your employees, present and future. Your plan tells them what you are trying to do with the business as well as their expected role. As obvious as you think your direction is, it isn't. Women tend not to think linearly. Think of your own life. One of the consequences of successfully juggling lots of things—kids, significant others, volunteer work, leisure time (okay, I exaggerate)—is that our employees often have little idea what we are trying to do with our company. A business plan tells them.

Your external audience is equally important. First in line is your banker or other investors. If you want to raise money for your firm a business plan is a must. Your service professionals, including your accountant, attorney, and insurance agent also need to see your plan. Why? Because they can also help you to get there from here by introducing you to potential clients and other business owners with whom you might be able to barter services (thereby saving money for other things) and supplies. I even share business plans with key suppliers so they will have patience with me later should I become a slow payer (because sales are going so well, of course).

Over time I have come to believe that starting or building a business without a business plan is like marrying someone after you've seen only their picture. You have the vision but don't know the details that will make it work.

PARTS

So what are the parts? Every plan has three: an executive summary, a body, and a financial section. You also need a cover sheet that tells your audience who the company is and your name, address, and telephone number. The cover sheet should include a statement that declares the document as confidential. Many years back I spent three years working with technology-based businesses to raise capital. I was always stunned at the number of business plans delivered to my office that had *no* contact name, let alone a telephone number, on the document. Moral of the story: Start a business plan with a cover page that looks something like this:

Example A

SENIOR MARKET SPECIALISTS
10032 Woodlawn Road
Detroit, MI 48140
(313) 476-5555

BUSINESS PLAN

* * *

This business plan has been prepared solely for the confidential use of selected individuals, companies, and organizations. It is intended only for the use of the person or entity to whom it is given and may not be distributed in part or in whole to any other person or entity without permission of Senior Market Specialists.

THE EXECUTIVE SUMMARY

Back to the main course: The real first part of the business plan is your executive summary. It is basically one to three pages long and contains the key points about your company that you would want people to read, knowing that you only have ninety seconds of their attention. The executive summary covers key milestones such as when you started, when you introduced your first product line -or when you will, how large you expect the company to grow, and so forth. If you are raising money for your company you want that information in the executive summary as well (that is, how much you are raising, why, and when it will be paid back).

I am a lazy writer so I actually save writing the executive summary until I've written the second part, the body of the plan. When the body is done, I read it, highlighting the key sentences. Then I pull those sentences out, squish them together, and I have an executive summary. Better yet, it actually tells the same story as the business plan and I didn't have to write anything new. You'll be able to tell when your executive summary is finished because it will start to read like a pretty good draft of a business brochure. When it does, you are done.

Example B

EXECUTIVE SUMMARY

Located in Detroit, Michigan, Senior Market Specialists provides on-call therapy to elderly people across the country who are dealing with loss. Using an 800 telephone number the firm contracts with psychiatrists and psychologists who are willing to make house calls on clients.

The company works in the following way: the 800 number will be available and manned 24 hours a day. The client calls the number and asks for help. Our "crisis team" staff then contacts, the therapist on call to give her the name of the client and the address so a visit can be immediately scheduled. Three psychologists, all located in Detroit, are on call at any one time.

The market for these services is significant. On any given day, as many as 10 percent of all elderly persons are trying to cope with loss. Added together, this market represents more than $100 million in the United States. Relative to its competition Senior Market Specialists has several significant market advantages. First, it is available 24 hours a day. This is important because loss is often most difficult to cope with at the end of a day or during a sleepless night. The therapists are all prescreened. Clients can pay for the service with credit cards or through insurance.

Senior Market Specialist is owned by Dr. Sharon Smith, a psychiatrist who practices out of Detroit Medical Center. Dr. Smith is planning to market the service through television advertisements in selected geographic target markets and two radio advertisements per day on the noon syndicated radio talk show, "And That's the Way I See It."

Senior Market Specialists is requesting $250,000 to cover the initial market testing for the period February 1994–July 1994.

THE BODY

The body of the plan should cover six topics: management, the background of the company, your products, your marketing plan, an action plan, and a risk analysis. There are no real rules about the actual order of these topics, in spite of what other authors say. As a woman, you need to be careful to spell out why your management team is the right team for your business. For example, many women hire their husbands to perform a specific management function. The plan needs to spell out why he is the appropriate person for that job. (If he isn't the right person, don't hire him. You will thank me later.) You can decide which topic is most important and write that section first. Some owners start with a description of the company, others start with their marketing section because they realize that unless there is a market and *they can prove it*, it doesn't make sense to write the rest of the plan. As I said, *you decide*.

Most women write business plans that are too long. And we use too many words. The best business plans are usually fifteen to twenty-five pages long—more than that and you've probably gone too far and said too much. Don't bother with full sentences unless you really need them. The more graphs, diagrams, and bulleted phrases you use, the easier digesting the document will be—both for your reader and for you when you go back to read the plan six months from now in an effort to remember what it was you said you planned to accomplish. You know—back when you were high on chocolate and the kids were taking naps. Back when you were sleeping more than six hours a night.

COMPANY DESCRIPTION

I'll describe the body in the order I normally use: *Company Description:* This includes your vision, the business you are in, and your expected milestones. It tells the reader the form of your business and whether you are incorporated, a partnership, or what. It is where you set your goals and objectives for the company. If you've been in business for awhile you can also describe your history. I call this section a broad brush stroke. It usually takes no more than several pages and sometimes only a paragraph or two. Be sure to say specifically why you think your business will succeed. You can prove your viewpoint through the other sections of the business plan. State it first here.

The biggest mistake most women make in this section is not describing what business we are really in. For example, instead of saying that we are in the business of making our clients' marketing efforts more successful, we say we are an advertising firm. While it's true that you want to state what you are (that is, an advertising firm) it's equally important to describe what the impact of that is on your clients (that is, their marketing efforts will finally work).

A second point here. This is a woman thing and I experience it all the time. It goes something like this. When I ask my male clients what their vision is for their company they usually tell me that in their first year they expect to sell their product with great success to the local market. In year two they will either cover the state or country; in year three either the country or international markets. *For the same business* a woman will tell me that her goal is the first year to sell locally; in year two she will also sell locally, and in year three she might expand to another metropolitan area. Now the result of these sex-differentiated visions has been fascinating. Although more men fail, the ones who succeed do ten times (or more) the business of a comparable female-owned business. *Take the risk* and stretch your vision.

Once you've described your vision and business to your satisfaction you can describe your products. You want to describe each product in detail. If you do this well your readers should be able to close their eyes and see it. A good business plan describes the advantages of each product relative to other products. Examples might be that your quality is higher or it could be more consistent or more easily available. Having raised money for companies for years I've learned the hard way that one of the differences between a good business plan and a *great* business plan is that a great business plan actually talks about the potential weaknesses of the products and what the owner can and will do to protect her company from those weaknesses. This feeds into that old business truism that what can go wrong will. Women who have thought through the potential problems are always better off than those who do not. This is not an easy task, especially since you will be spending much of your time defending what you think is right about the products, and here I am telling you to publicly identify the weaknesses.

What are examples of weaknesses? One might be that there are other products that look like yours—you need to figure out a way to differentiate yours in some way so others can find you in a crowd. Another weakness might be a dependency on one contract manufacturer—what happens if she gets hit by a truck? The process of writing the business plan will help you to think through these issues before you face them in real life. Think of it as sort of like premarital counseling—may the crisis never hit but if it does you'll be as ready as any smart business owner could be.

MANAGEMENT

Management comes next. The key facts that you need to communicate are the actual number and types of positions you are planning to create, the job description for each of these positions, and who will fill each slot.

Here is how I write this section: First I draw an organizational chart describing the "completed" company (that is, what the company will look like when it is all grown up—or three years from now—whichever happens first). In a corner of each box I write the year when the person filling the position will be or was hired.

I then use most of the area in the box to describe the functions of the job - in bullet form. If I have identified the person who will fill the position I write her name in the box. Underneath it I write several phrases that tell the reader why that person is appropriate for that particular position/job. The following example should help to explain what I'm trying to say here:

ORGANIZATION CHART

> **Mary Smith 1993**
>
> President
> - Strategic Planning
> - Financial Operations
>
> Ms. Smith was senior vice president of the XYZ Food Company for five years before she started Gourmets and Yen in 1991.

> **Jamie Markus 1993**
>
> Chief Financial Officer
> - Financial reporting
> - Bank relations

> *(Name)* 1993
>
> Vice President Marketing
> - Marketing strategy
> - Sales calls to Fortune 500 clients
> - Oversee sales staff

> *(Name)* 1993
>
> Plant Manager
> - Production operations
> - Inventory
> - Delivery

> *(Name)*
> 1994
> Sales
> Manager

> *(Name)*
> 1994
> Sales
> Manager

> *(Name)*
> 1994
> Production
> worker

> *(Name)*
> 1994
> Production
> worker

If I have people on my team who are not direct employees but will help me make my case—whatever that case is—I add them to the chart. For example, since you've found the best accounting firm, bank, and law firm to work with you, it may be worth adding them to the chart:

> ABC Accounting
> Kim Hogan,
> Firm Liaison

> DEF Law Firm
> Melinda Maple,
> Attorney

> Mary Jo Jefferson,
> President

> GHI Bank
> Linda Lutz,
> President

If you insist on a neat business plan you can also describe your staff in the following way:

Example C

PERSONNEL

President: Denise Beckley

The president of the company is responsible for all company objectives, planning, and operations. Functions covered by this position include:

• setting company policies and objectives, including marketing objectives.

- coordinating divisions and departments and establishing responsibilities and procedures for achieving objectives.
- overall coordination of supplies for production.
- overall coordination of any needed manufacturing tasks.
- all marketing activities including public-relation promotions and advertising.
- planning and directing sales programs including the hiring of representatives and attendance at trade shows.
- financial record keeping, including bookkeeping, billings, payables, taxes, and so forth.
- developing personnel policies and hiring and managing of staff, evaluating staff performance.
- reviewing activities and financial reports to determine progress in attaining objectives, revising objectives, and plans in accordance with current conditions.
- directing and coordinating fundings for operations.

Ms. Beckley has been in sales since 1974. Since that time she has started two successful retail operations, selling both at a profit within five years of start up. This is her third company.

Operations Assistant: Robert Bechtell

The operations assistant is responsible for taking and filling orders, tracking inventory, billings, and any secondary manufacturing that needs to be done to finish the products prior to sale. Functions covered by the operations assistant include:

- assisting with the coordination of production, distribution, and warehouse.
- keeping track of items purchased, costs, delivery, product performance, and inventories.
- taking orders and tracking them.
- day-to-day bookkeeping.
- monitoring of quality (quality control).
- conferring with customers and representatives to evaluate and promote improvements in products.

- office management: coordinating supplies, mail, customer calls unrelated to the products, overseeing the general functioning of the office.

Mr. Bechtell has been responsible for assisting the president since 1991. Prior to that he was operations manager for BB&L Enterprises for five years.

Sales Staff (to be hired)

Functions covered by this position include:

- finding and following up on customer leads.
- sales calls.
- attendance at trade shows.
- servicing appropriate customer needs related to product sales (for example, advice on displays).
- coordinating sales promotions.

Warehouse Staff (to be hired)

Functions covered by this position include:

- loading, unloading, and moving materials in and out of the warehouse.
- counting, weighing, quality testing, and recording the number of units handled on a daily basis.
- packaging products for delivery to customers and representatives.

Director of Marketing and Public Relations (to be hired)

Functions covered by this position include:

- advertising campaign and press release.
- public relations.
- all packaging design.

In 1995 the company will add a Chief Financial Officer of financial operations. The Chief Financial Officer will be responsible for strategic planning for the company.

I put resumes into an appendix and leave spaces blank if I haven't yet named someone to a specific position.

If you have any management information or communication systems that help to explain why you will be successful you can describe them in this section as well. The actual chart will show the reader how you've organized everyone and what their relationships are to one another so you do not need to write about those topics.

THE MARKET

Marketing: Women tend to do a good job on the marketing sections of their business plans. I've never quite figured out why. Maybe it's our penchant for detail or our historical socialization as people-pleasers.

Your main goal in this section is to convince the reader that you really have a market, (that is, customers who will buy your product). Men and women differ here. Men often figure out how big the whole market is and figure that if they just get 1 percent of it they will live happily ever after, and by the way how hard could it be to get 1 percent? When they start out my women clients tell me they've tried the product idea out on several of their friends who just loved it. (Right. I remember how all my friends just "loved" my husband until the day we were divorced after which he became an unforgivable bastard. Sound familiar?) Friends cannot provide legitimate market feedback. What you need is rational and random feedback, which you describe in this section.

Most marketing sections start with an environmental analysis, which is nothing at all the way it sounds. An environmental analysis is simply a description of the world around you—the economy, politics, technological trends, and demographic or people trends—and how those factors will probably impact your business. For example, looking at the economy you may want to talk about the growth in the Gross

Domestic Product (GDP—our one-number summary of how the economy is doing) and its negative impact on consumer behavior (that is, we are scared and want more warranties, guarantees, and the personal phone numbers of company presidents when we make a purchase). For the political arena you might want to write about any regulations that are impacting in your industry. People trends could include some statistics about potential customers—it 's to be hoped that there are increasing numbers of them out there and they all have more money. Technological trends are fairly straightforward. More and more technology emerges every day; more people use it; it is easier, smaller, and cheaper to use all the time.

Once you've described your context in no more than one or two pages you want to make some comments about your own industry (that is, what is going on, where growth is coming from, who the industry leaders are, and so forth).

Here is where the fun part begins. Who are your customers really? You cannot describe them in too much detail. You cannot know them too intimately. This is the most important part of your plan. Many times a summary profile such as the following one suffices to prove that there are people and/or companies who will buy your product.

If your customers are people a profile might look like this:

- Product: purchasers of self-help books on relationships
- Profile:
- Age: 20–50 years old, target 35–45 group
- Sex: women and men, target group—women
- Marital status: single but in a relationship; married; going through a divorce
- Income: $35,000 and up
- Education: some college

- Church: Protestant, Catholic, new-age-type churches, members of eastern religions (Zen)
- Geography: national
- Lifestyle: read books; have some alone time; may be seeing a counselor; under stress; multiple roles (wife, mother, career, etc.)
- Buying behavior: They buy books, impulsively, after a counseling session or support group meeting or when a friend tells them about the book; use Visa cards or checks to purchase books; buy books in malls downtown (as part of entertainment, or as a "small indulgence").

If your customers are companies a profile might look like this:

- Product: temporary personnel for engineering firms
- Profile: firm
- Type of company: any industry that uses engineers—automotive, transportation, aerospace industries
- Age of company: any age company; younger, growing companies more likely to hire temporaries
- Number of employees: companies with fewer than 500 employees
- Product line: companies that need engineers to work on just-in-time products
- Geographic area: Midwest states of Michigan, Ohio, Indiana, and Illinois
- Pertinent characteristics: Company has used temporary employees before, company experiencing growth.

If you sell to both people and companies both need descriptions. Your next task is to tell the reader why you know they will buy from you. In a paragraph or three I summarize any surveys I've taken, any past sales I've made, or (if it's all I have) secondary studies done by someone else that suggest that the population I've just profiled really will buy what I'm selling.

COMPETITION

There are several moments of truth when you write a business plan. The first occurs when you try to describe what business you are in. The second happens when you describe who will really buy your products. The third is when you take an honest look at your competition.

Everyone has competition. Everyone. The only business owners who don't have competition are those who haven't thought about the possibilities long enough. You have competition. That you do is partially good news. It at least proves that there is probably a market for your product. Your task is to figure out who your competition is and what their strengths and weaknesses are in the eyes of your customers. Again, this can best be done in the form of a chart:

Competition	Strength	Weakness
Name of competition		
Address		
Telephone #		

The following is an example of a competitive analysis.

COMPETITION

Senior Market Specialists faces four types of competition: "900" numbers; local therapists; family and friends; and books. The following chart summarizes the strengths and weaknesses of each from the perspective of the client.

1. "900" Numbers

Strengths: —Less expensive
              —Confidential
              —Convenient
              —Can be creative
              —Anonymous

Weaknesses: —Quality unproven
              —Trying to be all things to all people

2. Other Local Therapists

Strengths: —Nearby
              —Familiar
              —Nonverbal support available
                  (hugs, smiles, and so forth)

Weaknesses: —Clients have to go to them
              —Unavailable in moments of crisis
              —Have to meet face to face

3. Family/Friends

Strengths: —Sympathetic
              —Familiar
              —Available

Weaknesses: —Often have no idea what they are talking about;
                  can be dysfunctional, destructive to client
              —May not address exact problem
              —May not be available

4. Books

Strengths: —Available
              —Convenient
              —Inexpensive

Weaknesses: —No feedback
              —May not address exact problem
              —Can be difficult to understand

You want to talk about how much of the market each of your competitors controls and if their share is increasing or decreasing and why. Then you can talk about ways in which you might neutralize their strengths so customers will come to you first. Included might be your packaging, how you advertise, whether you take VISA, and if your software is in their language.

All your thoughts here are summarized in a market plan that describes:

- Your geographic objectives (that is, where you will sell your product). Remember to aim high.
- Your pricing policies.
- How you will serve your customers after they've purchased the product.
- All the different ways you will use to promote your products. This list can be as long and as creative as you can bear to be. Detail is important, as is attention to your budget. For example if you plan to market your product using flyers you need to describe how many flyers, where you will distribute them, and the information included on the flyer. If you are planning to go to trade shows, name them, place them, date them, and cost them out.
- How you will get the media to know you even exist.

At the end of the section you want to summarize the expected results of these efforts. For example you may expect special events to bring fifty people to your print shop, or if you advertise your seminar series three times in your local paper twenty people will register.

THE ACTION PLAN

Last lap. The action plan puts it all together in the form of a monthly chart. The more detail the better. Basically you want to list all the major chores that need to be done over the course of a year down a column on the left hand side of the page. On the right side you list all the months of the year and when (and by whom) each chore will be done.

Example:

Tasks to be Performed   M1 M2 M3 M4 M5 M6 M7 M8 M9 M10 M11 M12

An alternative layout of an action plan can be seen in the following example:

ACTION PLAN

1994

For the fiscal year, Tierra Fuega is concentrating on the completion of its product line and the start-up of sales. The company is also computerizing several functions, including inventory, sales, and its financial tracking system.

MILESTONES:	ACCOMPLISHED BY:
Completion of product lines	December 31, 1994
Computerization of inventory	December 31, 1994
Hiring sales staff (including distributors)	December 31, 1994
Financial management system in place	December 31, 1994
Policy manuals/staff policies (including benefits)	December 31, 1994
Sales-staff policy and sales manual in place	December 31, 1994
Sales training program	December 31, 1994

1995

For this fiscal year Tierra Fuega will continue to sell its existing product line, perform market feasibility studies on expanded products, and develop a prototype updated "one-stop shopping" distribution system.

MILESTONES:	ACCOMPLISHED BY:
Expand product line as appropriate	Ongoing
Increase sales staff as needed	Ongoing
Develop prototype "one-stop shopping"	June, 1995
Plan "roll-out" of national distribution system	December, 1995
Hire a sales manager for local and national sales	December, 1995
Hire a CFO/Strategic Planning executive	December, 1995
Integrate manufacturing into corp. headquarters	December, 1995

1996

Assuming a positive market reaction to the one-stop shop-ping distribution system, the major milestone for 1996 will be to fully integrate the system into five major markets: Detroit, Chicago, Cleveland, Florida, and Atlanta by June 1996.

If you plan to make your product yourself then you will need a fifth section, which describes your production process. Included are a step- by-step description of the process itself and *where* you'll make the product, how many of these things you can make, where you will buy your supplies (include your backup supplier), who will actually make the product, and what a typical production schedule looks like.

CONTINGENCY PLAN

Use your last surge of effort to think through a contingency plan. I remember working with a venture capitalist for years who had only one rule about success—he used to say that entrepreneurs who did not think through potential crises were doomed to failure. I agree. You want to take some time to think about the things that could go wrong in your business. List them and then think through the potential solutions to those problems so they can be listed as well. You can try using the format in the following example until you come up with one better suited to your business. Once you've written the contin-gency plan you can stop worrying about the things that could go wrong and go about the business of building your business. See the following example:

CONTINGENCY PLAN

RISKS	SOLUTIONS
Chief Executive Officer leaves	Both vice presidents have been trained in the overall operations of the firm. Either could take over if needed until a new CEO is located.
Can't find salespeople	Provide in-house training to enthusiastic newcomers to sales. Provide generous commissions for sales staff as an incentive for employment.
Packaging problems	Keep an ongoing file of reputable packaging companies for backup.
Production problems	Keep an ongoing file of reputable production companies for backup.
Sales are slower than expected	Postpone new product lines; cut product lines that aren't selling, postpone development of new distribution.
Company is sued	ABC Co. has a $4 million insurance policy as protection against customer lawsuits. We also have a guaranteed returns policy.

In many ways once you've written the body of your plan the hard part is done. The next step is to get a good accountant who can translate your story into numbers. That becomes the second major part of the plan. As you write the body of the plan you will make all sorts of assumptions about your business: how many staff you'll have, when sales will come in, the size of the sales, when your service providers will bill you and how much, and so forth. Listing them on a piece of paper that you've labeled "Assumption Page" as you think of them keeps you sane.

While it is true that we could translate those assumptions into a cash flow if we had to ourselves, for many women just thinking about it is agony enough. Don't think about how much money you'll save by doing your own numbers—you won't. Let a computer-smart, software-savvy accountant with a spreadsheet program you can understand prepare your financials.

How do you know when your business plan is finished? The first test is whether you've said all the things you had to say. The second test is that you can give the plan to someone who doesn't know and love you (everyone else is biased) to read. When that person can read the plan and then tell you exactly what you are trying to do with your business then you are done. Go buy yourself a present as a reward.

CHAPTER 7

*Y*OUR BUSINESS

IS NOT YOUR

FAMILY

(or)

MANAGING PEOPLE

No matter who you are, when you are in the room with her, (the president) acts as if you're the only person who matters. She makes you feel like her equal. She defers to you, cares about your opinions, gives you time to present your views. If there are other people present, even if you are a secretary or minor flunky, she treats you like the chairman of the board.
Mark McCormack

You are now in business. Your business plan is written. You have financing. The phone works. Customers are buying. More and more and faster and faster. It's time to get help. You literally need more bodies in the room to stay afloat. Who should they be? Where are they? How will you find them?

From *What They Still Don't Teach You at the Harvard Business School,* copyright © 1989 by Mark H. McCormack, Enterprises, Inc. Used by permission of Bantam Books, a division of Bantam Doubleday Dell Publishing Group, Inc.

125

FAMILY AND FRIENDS: PASS ON THE OPPORTUNITY

First, whom shouldn't you hire? The people closest to you. Why? Because you'll both go crazy. Here's the reason. People close to you may be willing to work long hours at low pay. But. Usually they see this as doing a favor for you. Even if they need a job and you have provided it, they see working for you as a favor. Either way, the end result is the same—from their perspective, you owe them. Vacations when they want it. A loan. Flexible hours. Day-care on demand. And, if you say no to their requests, if you don't pay them back, suddenly you have someone with a bad attitude (and you know what that's like), and just as quickly you face firing your sister or best friend. And it gets worse if you do fire her—or your dad because he just doesn't understand computers and you can't afford the time it takes for him to do your bookkeeping manually. The whole family will have an opinion regarding who is right and who is wrong. Now, overlay your situation with this truth: Americans are always for the underdog. Always. It's our culture. Looking at your situation, who is the underdog? Who will get the sympathy? Who will be the wicked witch of the east? Who will lose the support of the family? You. Whether or not you are in the right. Just when you need your family and friends behind you.

AND FORGET MATES

The case for mates is stronger. All the arguments about partnering with a mate are true here. Please, oh please, do not hire your mate. Why? Because you are changing. Rapidly. As you make decisions, you'll get better and better at making them. Your self-esteem will grow. You'll ask for feedback less and less. You'll also tolerate feedback less and less. You won't be the woman you were. Scary stuff to a mate. If you hire yours as an employee, you're asking that person to not only cope with—and applaud—your changes, you also expect him to take orders from you. An impossible task. It destroys relationships. In twelve years, I've seen mates work together successfully only three times. Each time, the man totally subordinated himself to the woman—in the relationship as well as in the business. You decide. The numbers tell the story. I wouldn't take the chance. A good mate is much harder to find than a good employee.

PEOPLE SKILLS: GENERALLY SPEAKING

Look at yourself first. To be a successful entrepreneur, you need to be a leader. You need to know how to motivate people, how to stay creative, and how to solve all sorts of problems on a continuing basis. Until recently, leadership models have revolved around the concept of a good coach. Successful women business owners have taught me that it's more than that. Thanks to them and thinkers like Stephanie Covey, we're learning that there is a better model. Lucky for you and me it's very female in its thrust, because it centers on people and relationships rather than on goals and objectives. In *Principle Centered Leadership,* Covey can guide you through the new paradigm. Here's what I pulled out for women business owners:

First, people will need to trust you. What you promise employees better happen. The same is true for your suppliers, service professionals, and banker. Second, the golden rule gets a new twist. You don't want simply to treat your employees as you want to be treated—you want to treat them in the same way that *you would treat your most respected customers.* And when you negotiate, know that if someone wins and another person loses, you'll be up the creek without a paddle—so you better hang in there until everyone is satisfied. Does this slow you down? You bet. Is it agonizing? It can be. Is it worth it? Every minute.

Third, it's okay to love your employees (not in the carnal way, unless you are ready for a rough-and-tumble roller coaster ride that always ends up in your throwing up all over yourself). I mean compassion. Caring that their lives are okay. (Although I'm not talking about solving their problems for them.) This is more important than people realize. George Mason University did a now-famous study in 1980 around the question of what motivates employees—which substantiates what I'm saying. Before I tell you what they found, take a couple of minutes to rank the following factors to see what you think motivates employees.

	HOW YOU THINK
FACTORS	**EMPLOYEES RANK THEM**
	(i.e. 1=most important,
	2=next most important, etc.)

Good working conditions
Feeling "in" on things
Job security
Promotion and growth
Good pay
Company loyalty to workers
Tactful discipline
Appreciation of work
Empathetic help on personal problems
Interesting work

Here's how the factors really were ranked. The three top motivating factors all had to do with relationships—with feeling as if someone cared about them. Number one was *appreciation of their work*. Think of all the jobs you've ever had. Were you ever appreciated enough? The second most important motivator was *feeling "in" on things*. Most managers, by the way, thought that would be number ten. The third most important motivator was empathetic help on personal problems. Employees want to be part of a community. They want to feel respected, as if they matter.

For the curious, here's the ranking for the rest of the factors: (4) job security, (5) good pay, (6) interesting work, (7) promotion and growth, (8) company loyalty to workers, (9) good working conditions, and (10) tactful discipline.

You need to be a leader. To have good people skills. The following chart gives you more clues.

ON BEING A LEADER: TIPS*

1. Don't act like a boss.
2. Recognize successes.
3. Ask for feedback—act on feedback.
4. Keep people informed.
5. Ask for ideas.
6. Stay close to your employees.
7. Tell the truth.
8. Listen to everyone.
9. Confront problems head on immediately.
10. Be proactive, not reactive.
11. Put yourself in your employees' shoes.
12. Inspect what you expect.
13. Be a role model.
14. Ask before you tell.
15. Encourage/reward innovation.
16. Do right.
17. Do your best.
18. Be consistent.
19. Be passionate about your business: "Passion" is contagious.
20. Have fun.
21. Share responsibility/enthusiasm/pride.
22. Trust yourself—trust others.
23. See every problem as an opportunity.
24. Admit when you're wrong.
25. Ask for help.
26. Acknowledge what you don't know.

---

*These tips were taken from a free half-day training program sponsored by Comerica Bank for their clients. Talk about relationship building. No wonder their customers stay.

Everyone you hire needs to have people skills too. What does that mean? On its broadest level, they should *like* people. A lot. This is not as obvious as it sounds—some people don't like others. Now is not the time to figure out why. Just don't hire them. How do good leadership skills manifest themselves? Mostly through a person's listening skills (that is, they know how to listen) and through their compassion (that is, they show concern for other people). People who will be good employees will show a willingness to hear feedback to improve their own skill set. Here's how I tell if someone has people skills. Every human interaction has two levels: human and business. A person with people skills always has both levels in his communication style. The human level is the part where we interact as people. It's the part of a conversation where you ask me how I am, how my week was, how am I feeling, and so forth. At this level, we are communicating respect for each other, our dignity, love for each other, compassion.

Every interaction should start and end with a human interaction for people to feel good about it. If the person you want to hire begins and ends conversations with a human element, people skills are probably a part of his or her personality. The business part of the conversation is what the conversation is actually about; for example, after you have checked in with someone, you may want to know if she's collected this month's bills. You can find out and then go back to the human interaction. For example, you may mention that you hope her week will go well. As an aside, when we women start our own businesses, we tend to forget how important the human element is in how we communicate. This happens because we are juggling more and more balls with less and less time. Our conversations become abrupt, to the point and, in our minds, very businesslike. This is deadly. Can you remember the last time you had someone walk into your house to say "When's dinner?" With no kind words before or after the question? Do you remember your reaction? Wasn't it anger? For most people it would be. Why? Because there is no human element in the interaction. The scenario doesn't matter. What matters is remembering that there are two people interacting—two people with human needs who want to be cared about, to be in a relationship with each other at some level. Checking in shows us we are in that relationship.

Watch for this skill of understanding in any potential team member.

WHEN TO HIRE: A CHECKLIST

How can you tell when you need to think about hiring help? Fortunately, there are obvious signs. The main one is that you find yourself needing to be in two places at once all the time. To my knowledge, only the naked religious ascetics in 2500 B.C. really knew how to pull this trick off (in spite of what my new-age friends tell me). You'll know if this is a problem without anyone else needing to tell you. In my experience, waiting to hire someone until you always need to be in two places at once is waiting too long. So what are other clues that will tell you that it's time?

The following checklist should help you to decide it's time. As you read it, you might want to check those that apply to you right now to see how close you are to your hiring years:

☐ 1. You have no time to prepare for (not to mention even think about) unexpected calamities.

☐ 2. You feel stretched too thin—all the time. It is as though nothing can ever be done as well as you wish, because you simply don't have the time. Follow-up phone calls don't get made, and you can't remember the last time you made it through your "to do" list.

☐ 3. You are always running out of things—supplies, space, inventory, equipment.

☐ 4. Your day-to-day activities are greatly speeded up—as a result, you feel frenzied most of every day.

☐ 5. There are more and more crises as things get lost through the cracks.

☐ 6. Even though sales are increasing, you start to wonder if it's all worth it.

If more than two of these statements are true for you, it's time to think seriously about getting help in the form of employees. The majority of us can cope with one or two of the problems and still live to talk about it, but more than that will make you crazy.

Now, most company owners make an assumption that once they need help, the only option is full-time staff. Wrong. All sorts of scenarios are possible, ranging from bringing in a couple of bright teenagers several afternoons a week, to sharing a bookkeeper with another firm, to leasing a full-time employee or employees.

Once you've admitted to yourself that you need help (an agonizing decision for all entrepreneurs, because it means giving up control, and we *hate* to do that), the next step is to figure out how much help you can afford.

Look at your cash flow. If you have sufficient income to cover your operations (rent, utilities, supplies, insurance, your salary, and marketing and sales costs) and there is still money in the bank, it's time to hire help. Don't start with full-time help until you are certain that you really need it. The last thing you want is to fork out a full-time salary to someone who doesn't have enough work to do. They hate it (although no one admits it, people hate boredom more than stress) and so will you.

To my mind, there is a continuum of hiring that should take place. The first step is to get the bookkeeping out of your life. Why? Because accounting-related work is tedious and detail-driven and entrepreneurs aren't. Find a *reputable* bookkeeping service if you can. Most accounting firms offer some form of bookkeeping service, and there are some excellent independent bookkeeping services around. Or you can hire a part-time bookkeeper who can come in once or twice a week to help. Once you have someone to help you with your books, you need to give that person or system some time—usually several weeks—to see how much of a load she's taken off your shoulders.

If, at the end of a month, you would still go back to the when-to-hire checklist and mark off more than two of the problems, it's time for step two: getting office help.

There are lots of choices here. My favorite is to find two (so they can cover each other when one has exams or a date or a game or anything else that the young feel obligated to do) smart and competent high school or college students to come in several afternoons a week to help—like Wednesday and Thursday, so you have Monday to plan and start your week and Friday to clean up after yourself.

Again, give them several weeks to kick into gear and then go over the checklist again to discover whether more hiring is appropriate. Step three is to find a half-time receptionist/office manager who can sweep up behind you as needed. Don't formally hire that person yet. Instead, try using a temporary agency to supply a half-time office worker to see how the hours work out. Although the agency's hourly rate might be higher than if you hired someone directly, a temporary service allows you to stop using the person without guilt or additional costs of firing if you find that you simply don't need that much assistance. On the other hand, you may find that you need even more help. Try a full-time temp. Keep exploring until you figure out *how many hours* of help you need before deciding among full- and part-time options.

Once you know the hours, you can face the moment of truth. Should you hire a person or lease that person? If you decide to hire a person—whether she is full- or part-time—be prepared for paperwork. A good accountant can talk you through the forms you need to fill out. The following list is a preview.

WHEN YOU HIRE: PAPERWORK OBLIGATIONS

1. State and federal taxes. You need to register with the Internal Revenue Service (1-800-829-1040) and your state for social security tax and income tax withholding for your employees. These taxes must be withheld from each employee's wages and paid to the appropriate taxing agency. Some cities levy a city income tax. Contact the City Treasurer's Office for information.

2. State unemployment insurance. You need to register with your state's Employment Security Commission (or the equivalent) for unemployment tax purposes. Unemployment taxes are paid by the employer—no deduction is allowed from any employee's wages.

3. Federal unemployment insurance. You need to pay federal unemployment taxes. Contact the Internal Revenue Service (1-800-829-1040) for information. Unemployment taxes are paid by the employer—no deduction is allowed from any employee's wages.

4. Worker's compensation. Most employers are required to provide worker's compensation coverage for their employees. A worker's compensation policy is purchased from your private insurance company.

5. Health and safety standards. Employers must comply with health and safety standards under federal and state Occupational Safety and Health Acts (OSHA) and Right-to-Know laws. Call your state's Department of Labor for information.

6. Immigration law compliance. All employers must verify the employment eligibility of all employees hired after

November 6, 1986, by reviewing documents presented by employees and recording the information on a verification form. Call your governor's office to find out who is responsible for this in your state.

7. Minimum wage. Federal and state regulations set minimum wage and overtime standards. Contact the U.S. Department of Labor for help on this one.

8. Age restrictions. Employers hiring anyone under the age of eighteen should be aware of restrictions on the type of work they can do, hours they can work, and the need for a work permit. Contact your state's Department of Labor.

9. Employee information. Employers are also required to display certain posters in the work place. Following is a list of the required posters and where they can be obtained: Federal Minimum Wage—contact the U.S. Department of Labor. Equal Employment Opportunity—contact U.S. Equal Employment Opportunity Commission (202-634-6922) for federal forms. Your state might also have forms. Employee Polygraph Protection Act—contact the U.S. Department of Labor, Wage and Hour Division.

In Michigan, for example, all employers need to fill out and file MESC-1009 registration, which the state then uses to determine the firm's liability for Michigan's unemployment taxes. The second form you need to fill out is the C-3400, which registers your firm with the state for sales and use taxes, the state withholding tax, and the single business tax. Your state will have comparable forms. You are also required to have a worker's compensation insurance policy, which you can purchase from a knowledgeable insurance agent. Even in situations where you decide to formally hire someone, it's best to start out with a fairly short contract. My favorite is six months. If the person works out and you can afford to keep her, you can always renew the contract.

On the other hand, if she doesn't, you know that, at worst, you have to survive her for only six months.

Another option is to lease your employees. In this case, you still find the person you want but the leasing company formally hires her and "leases" her back to you. As a result, you don't have all the forms and paperwork associated with hiring staff. If you hate paperwork or simply don't have time, you might want to consider this. While it is true that there is some cost for using a "third party," the leasing industry is growing rapidly, suggesting that more and more entrepreneurs are deciding to go that route.

FINDING THE RIGHT STAFF

How do you find the right people? By being careful about what you want. Never hire anyone without developing a job description first. A good job description has two parts. The first is a list of the actual responsibilities of the job. For example, if you are going to hire an office manager, the job responsibilities will probably include:

- Coordinate schedules for staff.
- Hire receptionist.
- Hire secretaries.
- Manage receptionist and secretaries.
- Purchase office supplies.
- File key documents.
- Produce and mail reports on a timely basis.
- Ensure financial reports completed on time on a weekly basis.
- Coordinate the upkeep of the computers.

The second part of the job description is a translation of those responsibilities into skill requirements. At a minimum, the office manager will need the following skills:

- Organizational

- People skills (she likes people, can communicate well, includes two communication levels when she talks to people, etc.)
- Ability to make deadlines
- Computer skills
- Understanding of financial reports
- Problem solving

You can't afford to make a mistake—the cost of mis-hires is high, both in terms of money and time. The best entrepreneurs recruit all the time, even when they may not have an opening. Constantly watch for good people, including those who are already employed. In an excellent article on hiring in the February 1992 issue of *Inc.* magazine, Tom Garrison, a Dallas food broker, says, "We are looking for people who aren't looking for a job—they're happy and productive where they are. When we find that person, we try to sell him on why he should work here. . . ." According to the article, when Garrison runs across someone he thinks he'd love to have as an employee, or conversely, that he himself would like to work for, he engages her in a conversation about his industry. "If she's excited, if we see she's reading us, then we move into why Brown, Moore & Flint is a good place to work."

And while I'm at it, never hire someone without interviewing him several times. The folks at Zingerman's, an Ann Arbor deli made famous by *Esquire* and *Inc.*, interview people three times. Applicants not only fill out forms, they perform tests to demonstrate their math and office skills, and they are interviewed by both key managers and the president of the company.

Prior to any interview, it's worth your time to consider what questions will best help you to discover whether you've found the right person. Chart I is a form I've used successfully when interviewing new people. It lays out job responsibilities, skill requirements, some questions that can help you get to the skill requirements, and a system for ranking a candidate that gives you a measurable way to choose between candidates.

CHART I

Job Responsibilities: Office Manager

- Coordinate schedules for staff.
- Hire receptionist and secretaries.
- Ensure fully staffed.
- Manage receptionist and secretaries.
- Purchase supplies
- File key documents.
- Ensure financial reports completed on time on a weekly basis.
- Produce/mail reports on a timely basis.
- Coordinate upkeep of computers.

Skills Require-ments	Questions	Answers	Rank of Each Skill	Rating (1-10) (of candidate on each skill)	Overall Score (multiply rating × rank)
Organiza-tional	Tell me about projects you have coordinated in the past.				
People skills	How do you hire people? Give me an example of a time when you had to resolve a conflict between two people.				
Deadline sensitivity	What did you do when you knew you couldn't meet a deadline on a project?				
Computer skills	Describe your computer skills. Are you familiar with (a certain type of software)? What do you do when a computer quits on you?				
Under-standing of finan-cial reports	Have you had an account-ing class? Have you dealt with finan-cial reports before? When? Tell me how you would ex-plain these financial reports to someone who doesn't un-derstand them.				

Chart II is a list of sample questions that are also good lead-ins shared with me by the Comerica Bank staff.

CHART II
SAMPLE INTERVIEW QUESTIONS

Remember: Good questions focus on *skills* and *job responsibilities*.

1. How good are your listening skills? How do you know?
2. Tell me about a time when you had to organize a project and had a tight deadline.
3. We've all had times when we misunderstood something important. Give me some examples of when this happened to you and why.
4. We've all had to say no to customers in the course of business. Give me an example of when you have had to do this and how you handled it.
5. If I were to ask your previous co-workers to describe you, what would they tell me?
6. If I were to ask your former boss (or teacher, etc.) to name the one area that you most need to work on, what would he or she tell me?
7. What characteristics do you think are important in being an excellent _____ (fill in job title)?
8. *How would you rate yourself* on those characteristics on a scale of 1-10? Why?
9. We have all had a disagreement with our bosses. Give me an example of a disagreement you have had and how you have handled it.
10. What are your personal standards of excellence? How do you know when you have done a good job?
11. Give me an example of a time when you were working in a stressful situation. How did you handle it?
12. What are one or two of the best ideas you've ever had?
13. How do you typically approach obstacles to getting the job done?
14. Tell me about a time when _____.
15. Give me an example of when you've _____.
16. What's happened when you've _____.

Warning. There are many questions that you *cannot ask by law*. Unfortunately, they aren't as obvious as you might expect. The following list summarizes the dos and don'ts according to the Michigan Department of Civil Rights. Call your governor's office to get one for yourself and *be careful*. Thousands of well-meaning employers have found themselves in hot water because they've asked well-meant but illegal questions. Here's an example. You cannot ask someone if he or she owns a car. You can only ask if he or she has access to a car. Seems trivial, but it isn't from the perspective of civil rights.

CHART III: WHAT CAN YOU ASK?
Preemployment Inquiry Guide

Subject	Lawful Preemployment Inquiries	Unlawful Preemployment Inquiries
NAME:	Applicant's full name. Have you ever worked for this company under a different name? Is any additional information relative to a different name necessary to check work record? If yes, explain.	Original name of an applicant whose name has been changed by court order or otherwise. Applicant's maiden name.
ADDRESS OR DURATION OF RESIDENCE:		
BIRTHPLACE:		Birthplace of applicant. Birthplace of applicant's parents, spouse, or other close relatives. Requirement that applicant submit birth certificate, naturalization, or baptismal record.

Subject	Lawful Preemployment Inquiries	Unlawful Preemployment Inquiries
AGE:	*Are you 18 years old or older?	How old are you? What is your date of birth?
RELIGION OR CREED:		Inquiry into an applicant's religious denomination, religious affiliations, church, parish, pastor, or religious holidays observed.
RACE OR COLOR:		Complexion or color of skin.
PHOTOGRAPH:		Any requirement for a photograph prior to hire.
HEIGHT:		Inquiry regarding applicant's height.
WEIGHT:		Inquiry regarding applicant's weight.
MARITAL STATUS:	Is your spouse employed by this employer?	Requirement that an applicant provide any information regarding marital status or children. Are you single or married? Do you have any children? Is your spouse employed? What is your spouse's name?
SEX:		Mr., Miss, or Mrs. or an inquiry regarding sex. Inquiry as to the ability to reproduce or advocacy of any form of birth control.
HEALTH:		Inquiries regarding an individual's physical or mental condition that are not directly related to the requirements of a specific job and that are used as a factor in making employment decisions.

Requirement that women be given pelvic examinations. |

Subject	Lawful Preemployment Inquiries	Unlawful Preemployment Inquiries
CITIZENSHIP:	Are you a citizen of the United States?	(The following questions are unlawful unless asked as part of the Federal I-9 process.)
	If not a citizen of the United States, does applicant intend to become a citizen of the United States?	Of what country are you a citizen?
	If you are not a United States citizen, have you the legal right to remain permanently in the United States?	Whether an applicant is naturalized or a native-born citizen; the date when the applicant acquired citizenship.
	Do you intend to remain permanently in the United States?	Requirement that an applicant produce naturalization papers or first papers.
	(To avoid discrimination based on national origin, the preceding questions should be asked after the individual has been hired, even if it is related to the Federal I-9 process.)	Whether applicant's parents or spouse are naturalized or native-born citizens of the United States; the date when such parent or spouse acquired citizenship.
NATIONAL ORIGIN:	Inquiry into languages applicant speaks and writes fluently.	Inquiry into applicant's (a) lineage; (b) ancestry; (c) national origin; (d) descent; (e) parentage, or nationality, unless pursuant to the Federal I-9 process.
		Nationality of applicant's parents or spouse.
		What is your mother tongue?
		Inquiry into how applicant acquired ability to read, write, or speak a foreign language.

Subject	Lawful Preemployment Inquiries	Unlawful Preemployment Inquiries
EDUCATION:	Inquiry into the academic, vocational or professional education of an applicant and the public and private schools attended.	
EXPERIENCE:	Inquiry into work experience.	
	Inquiry into countries applicant has visited.	
ARRESTS:	Have you ever been convicted of a crime?	Inquiry regarding arrests that did not result in conviction (except for law enforcement agencies).
	Are there any felony charges pending against you?	
RELATIVES:	Names of applicant's relatives, other than a spouse, already employed by this company.	Address of any relative of applicant, other than address (within the United States) of applicant's father and mother, husband or wife, and minor dependent children.
NOTICE IN CASE OF EMERGENCY:	Name and address of person to be notified in case of accident or emergency.	Name and address of nearest relative to be notified in case of accident or emergency.
MILITARY EXPERIENCE:	Inquiry into an applicant's military experience in the Armed Forces of the United States or in a State Militia.	Inquiry into an applicant's general military experience.
ORGANIZATIONS:	Inquiry into the organizations of which an applicant is a member, excluding organizations the name or character of which indicates the race, color, religion, national origin, or ancestry of its members.	List all clubs, societies, and lodges to which you belong.
REFERENCES:	Who suggested that you apply for a position here?	

*This question may be asked only for the purpose of determining whether applicants are of legal age for employment.

Once you have your questions and ask them, listen. Listen hard to the interviewee's responses and how she is saying them. Watch for attitude. All the skills in the world won't make up for a poor work attitude. Ever. Watch how a person interacts with other people, such as a waitress or waiter if you take the applicant to lunch. Find out how she responds to stress. Look for someone smarter than you. Find out how much pay she needs to feel respected. I've had several wonderful mentors I've hired as my own staff. One of the best was a venture capitalist from Grand Rapids who taught me that every potential employee should get interviewed at least three times in at least three different environments—hers, yours, and one that scares the heck out of her. It is a process similar to one he used to decide about investing in a company. He used to use the first interview to build rapport and learn about the person generally. The second interview served to teach the potential staff person about his firm and the job. He would also use the second interview to discover something that caused stress for the person—like his golf game, or sailing, or racquetball. Then he would take that person into the stressful environment because it showed how the interviewee would respond to difficult situations. While his wasn't a fail-safe interview system, it came very close.

PARTNERING

Once you've identified your staff, forget managing them. People don't want managers, they want partners. Think about it. You can go to any group of people and ask them what comes to mind when you say the word "manager." They'll spit back words like "referee," "delegator," "baby-sitter," "enforcer," even "terminator." If you use the word partner, the words shift dramatically to "sharing," "cooperation," "openness," "communicator," and "resource broker." They are more positive, more optimistic.

Be a partner. Once you have staff, help them to learn how to tell what actions of theirs will lead to the objectives they're after. Chart IV is an example of a tracking sheet for a bookkeeper. The action steps become an actual "to do" list for your staff. Commit to reviewing the goals list weekly for employees when they first join you. It doesn't matter whether your staff is made up of temporaries, part-timers, leased employees or permanent employees. The exercise is the same.

CHART IV

JOB RESPONSIBILITIES (This comes from you.)	OBJECTIVES (This comes from them.)		ACTIONS/STEPS (This comes from both of you.)
	Tasks	Done By	
Reconcile cash situation	Balance completely	Daily	Post all entries Total balances Reconcile differences
Place collection calls	Maintain accounts (under 30 days)	Daily	Identify delinquent accounts Confirm balances for recent collections Place call requiring action step
Prepare/mail invoices	Invoices sent (within 24 hours)	Daily	Review invoice for dollar accuracy Post to books Confirm addresses Mail

NEGOTIATION SKILLS

What if you don't end up with the behavior you expected from your staff? Here's where negotiation skills come in.

The book that helped me to best understand the process of negotiating is *Getting Past No: Negotiating with Difficult People* by William Ury. The reason I like it is because whenever I have to negotiate anything—salaries, bedtimes, the cost of fixing my brakes—to my mind the other person is being difficult. If she weren't difficult, I wouldn't be negotiating in the first place!

In a perfect situation, both people would know exactly what they want and agree to negotiate to a win-win. Unfortunately, we're not perfect. Neither are the situations we find ourselves in as business owners. When an employee isn't meeting your expectations, it's time to stop to straighten her and you out because these situations only get worse. Here are three things that don't work:

1. *Ignoring the problem.* It never goes away unless you negotiate it away.

2. *Labeling the person.* "He's too stupid." "She's too slow." Labels are destructive.

3. *Mind reading.* We women love to do this. This is the pretend art of guessing what is going on internally in someone else. So we have an explanation in our minds for why they are acting the way they are. "He's late every morning because he's under a lot of stress." "She didn't do the books correctly because she is having her period." Mind reading is deadly. First of all, we're usually wrong as often as we are right. Secondly, it doesn't change any behavior.

You need to negotiate for the behavior you want. Fortunately, there are very clear steps in a negotiation process:

Step 1: *Define the problem.* State the situation, how it is, and how it needs to be. For example, if you walk in and the office is a mess, you can say, "Judy, this office is a mess. There's dirt on the floor, the garbage can is full, and I can write my name in the dust on the bookcase. It's important for the office to be clean so our customers feel comfortable." Don't assume that people already know what their expectations are.

Step 2: *Learn what is behind his or her behavior.* Let the person tell his story first. The whole story. Without interruptions. Ask for his input. What is your staff person's view of the situation? What does he think is going on? For example, his response to the messy office might be, "I didn't know how important this was to you. I've been spending my whole time getting your client reports out on time." *Find out the reason why the situation exists.* Here you paraphrase back what your employee just said. For example, "So the reason is that you have been getting those reports out . . ." Hang in there and keep paraphrasing until he says "yes." Don't argue about who is right. Ever. Such showdowns only make each of you angry and lock you into defensive behavior where you use all your energy to prove that the other person is wrong. Nothing is really gained, because in our own minds we're always right no matter what the other person says. And the more someone else tells us we're wrong the more right we become. There are only three reasons that I know for poor job performance: (1) don't know how, (2) I don't know what the expectations are, and (3) I don't care. It's up to you to discover which of these is at work.

Step 3: *Explain the consequences of the behavior.* People need to know what will happen if they don't perform—to them, to you, to the company. "If the report continues to be late, someone else will have to do it." "If you don't get those collections, we won't earn our commissions." "If I hear on the street what we've discussed, I'll know that I can no longer trust you." "We have certain procedures in the firm. If they aren't followed, this could lead to termination."

Step 4: *Negotiate a solution.* This may mean repeating steps one through three over and over until you really know what is going on. What can be done to remedy the situation? It's best for the staff person to come up with a solution. Wait. Be patient. Let her come up with a suggestion first. Be honest. Keep going until you have an agreed-upon solution to the problem.

There are some clear ground rules to Step 4, since this is, in many ways, your make-it-or-break-it step.

A. *Don't react.* As I think of this, staying "unreactive" in a session like this is one of the most difficult things you'll do as a business owner. Why? Because human beings are reaction machines. We want to defend all of our actions—all the time. Reactions don't work. Fighting fire with fire just makes you both mad. (The one I hear most is, "You said you would . . . and you didn't . . ." We all want to respond with something like, "When did you do what you promised?" or something worse.) Don't defend. Detach from the emotions of the moment. Yes, this will take some practice. The only way I know how to do it is to keep reminding myself of how hard it was to find this person in the first place and that it may be much easier (and certainly cheaper!) to improve her behavior rather than to start the hiring process all over again. The more restrained you are the less resistance you'll get—to you and to the process.

If you start to get angry:

- Count to ten. Or twenty. Or a hundred.
- Breathe deeply.
- Slow the conversation down and review it quietly with the other person.
- Stay focused.
- Take a break.

B. *Disarm her.* In other words, get her respect. The way to do this is through surprise—don't do what she expects. Do the opposite. Such as:

- Being able to repeat word for word what was just said.
- Acknowledging her points.
- Agreeing whenever and wherever you can.
- Sitting beside her.
- Taking a break to get some food or chocolate together.
- *Not interrupting.*
- Waiting until she is done speaking and asking, "Is there anything else?"
- Saying "I'm sorry"—as in, "I'm sure this has been frustrating for you."

C. *Give him the opportunity to be in your shoes.* Ask what your staff would do in your situation. Define the problem again and ask for potential solutions. Try all kinds of options—"what ifs." Remember that we humans are more apt to follow through when we come up with our own solutions and plans. It's our nature. Let him come up with the solution. And it's okay to be quiet when you need to think. Make it as easy as possible to come up with a solution. You can't push, cajole, or apply too much pressure here. It won't work. It's better to keep asking "what ifs" until you come up with something that will work for both of you. And don't be afraid to remind him of the consequences of no solution. He will no longer be an employee.

Step 5: *Follow up.* If the problem was important enough to bring up in the first place, it's important enough to follow through to resolution. Keep working with your staff. Keep describing the situation honestly as you plan out the solution. If it isn't fixed, don't say it is. Keep negotiating for changed behavior until the problem is resolved. Don't stop. Shifting gears is difficult and time consuming, yet that is just what you asked your staff to do. You both need to agree on how you'll track changes—so you'll both know what is working and what isn't.

What happens when the employee just won't take responsibility for the solution—no matter what—or when you negotiate a solution but nothing changes? Then it's time to think about firing.

FIRING

Nothing is fun about firing. The first time I fired someone I waited way too long—until everyone on my staff knew I had a liar on my hands, someone who was jeopardizing the entire business. It didn't help that this was an older gentleman who had a wife at home and two kids in college. The day I let him go (his words to me—"What took you so long?"), I went home, cried for two hours, and stayed in bed with a pillow over my head until the next morning. It was awful. Right down there with divorce.

You already know the best preventative measures: hiring carefully, finding people smarter than you, paying them well, respect, and so forth. Unfortunately, there are no guarantees. Life situations change. People discover drugs and alcohol. You may find staff who simply cannot work for a woman, even though they want to. The company may outgrow someone's skill set. The job description needs to change and they can't.

Firing is awful. It's failure in your face. It means you made a wrong decision. Publicly. With serious consequences. As a business owner, you'll need to face up to the problem and just do it. How?

Start with making sure that you have *early-alarm systems* for everyone on your staff. May you never need them. But if you do, they'll be there. An early-warning system is a performance appraisal where you sit down to discuss your staff's progress. Use these often; they'll keep both of you posted. I also like to see weekly performance summaries of some form. This can be as creative as you want it to be. A checklist of actions taken works; so does a copy of their weekly day timer. I have a client who has his salespeople daily FAX him the names and addresses of all the people they called on, the results of the meetings, and the next steps. It's a great running summary—he rarely needs to see his people face to face.

More and more companies are using benchmarking. In her *Inc.* article on *How to Fire* (May 1992), Ellyn E. Spragins describes how powerful an early-alarm-system benchmarking is. "At Datatec, benchmarking prevails. Datatec measures everything—defects in receivables, late orders, length of service calls, you name it. It also requires all employees to rate everyone else's performance either monthly or quarterly. And it surveys customers for their opinions. The results are published monthly for everyone in the company to see. So imagine this: After a week of training, you, the new guy at Datatec, start being graded at the end of your first month. You see immediately how you rank on every aspect of your job. It's obvious where you need to improve. Because the surveys are so frequent, problems are caught early and better performance shows up immediately. And because managers are using the same survey results as workers to evaluate performance, differences in perception are minimized. The strength of Datatec's system is that it allows employees to correct themselves."

When a problem arises, you already know how to try to negotiate a solution. If you can't, *don't delay*. Fire the person. Carefully. Why? Because people are suing former employers right and left for wrongful termination. In the last twenty years, these suits have increased by 2,000 percent. How can you protect yourself? By doing four things:

1. *Don't wait to deal with a problem when it shows its face.* If you're tracking employees closely, you'll notice problems quickly. Deal with them. Solve them. Include the employee in the solution. Get his or her buy-in, even if the solution is perceived as a "have to."

2. *Document everything.* You need a written track record of your problem-solving efforts. Be detailed. What did you say? What did she say? What solution(s) did you try? What are specific examples of the problem? On principle, I share my documentation with the employee so there are no surprises later. Since I've had personnel files stolen from my office (a disgusting but fairly common problem, I've discovered), I keep a second file off premises.

3. *Have a company policy about the firing procedure and follow it.* Write the policy now. Include how many warnings people get. I give staff three warnings (or tries) because (a) that's how I was raised and (b) I'm a wimp. You decide what

matches your personality best and document it in writing, as part of a larger personnel policy. Then use it. And document your use.

4. *Fire someone face to face.* In front of a witness. In privacy. I always tell people exactly why they are being fired—verbally and in writing. It always has to do with job performance. Anything else will lead to trouble for you . . . big time trouble. So, if attitude is a problem, it needs to be related to job performance. It needs to feed into a job description that included a "strong, positive work attitude," which is explained as "a willingness to be helpful, a courteous and pleasant demeanor" . . . or however you want to define it. While a bad attitude is almost impossible to document, proving it through written examples of someone coming to work late or constantly arguing with many other employees or turning in sloppy work aren't.

In an exit interview, I deliver the bad news, answer any questions the employee has, and explain any company policies I may have related to firing someone. The most important concerns are:

- Severance pay? Will he get any, what amount and for how long?

- Help finding next job? Will you actually help her? If yes, what will you do? Will you call associates yourself, hire an outplacement firm to help? What? What will you say when people call for references?

- Health benefits? Follow the law. It's constantly changing. I expect that it won't be long before all employers are obligated to provide health benefits (assuming you are already providing them) for several months for terminated employees. You need to spell out exactly what you are going to provide—in writing. Then provide it.

- Unemployment benefits? Again, it's important here to follow the law. My tendency is to do what I can to allow for a fired employee to receive unemployment benefits. He needs to eat. Tell the employee your decision and know that if you are firing him and are not planning to support the payment of unemployment benefits you will probably have a serious fight on your hands.

- What could you have done better? This is no time for false pride. Now is the time to find out what went wrong from the employee's perspective. You'll never get more honest feedback. Try to listen with detachment and take notes so you can go over their comments in a calmer moment. I always want to know what the fired employee thought of working with me, how he or she felt about the work environment, and any advice to make things easier for a replacement. Remember, owning a business is a life-long learning process. The more you learn, the more successful you will be.

Once we've had the face-to-face meeting, I like to escort the employee out the door as quickly as possible. For everyone's sake. Because it's time to move on. For everyone. It's also a good idea to talk to any other employees face to face (or in a group meeting if you have a lot of employees) to let them know what happened—sticking to facts and not opinions. Most important, use that conversation to assure people that they aren't next (unless they are) and to remind them how valuable an asset they are to you and to the firm. Show them, too. Use courtesy, patience, concern, and a willingness to hear their perspective of what happened if they need to tell you.

DON'T FORGET

As you settle into your new role as an employer, don't forget what it's like to be an employee. Keep the chart below to remind you of employees' priorities.

	Percent of Workers Who	
	Ranked It as Very Important	Said They Were Satisfied
Good health insurance and other benefits	81	27
Interesting work	78	41
Job security	78	35
Opportunity to learn new skills	68	31
Having a week or more of vacation	66	35
Being able to work independently	64	42
Recognition from co-workers	62	24
Regular hours (no weekends, no nights)	58	40
Having a job in which you can help others	58	34
Limiting job stress	58	17
High income	56	13
Working close to home	55	46
Work that is important to society	53	35
Chances for promotion	53	20
Contact with a lot of people	52	45
Flexible hours	49	39

Source: Gallup Poll, Princeton, NJ, 1991

CHAPTER 8

MANAGING THE WORLD OF YOUR BUSINESS

PART II: YOUR TIME

START BY SETTING PRIORITIES

You'll want to do everything. Everything. Because no one alive today can do anything you need done as well as you can. Well, you can't. Do everything, that is. You have only twenty-four hours in your day, and once they kick in businesses need more than that. They need more people doing more things.

The implications of this truth are serious. It means that you will first have to admit that you can't do everything. A corollary point: You also can't have everything.

If the 1970s and 1980s taught us any real lesson, it's that we can't do everything. We tried. And now there's a whole generation of glazed-over men and women trying to remember what it was they wanted—too exhausted even to try for part of it anymore. The indicators are everywhere. More people living alone. Because trying to find and keep relationships was too exhausting with everything else we were trying to manage. More people dropping out. Is it just my friends or are lots of baby boomers and post-yuppies bidding the All-American dream good-bye? Last night a friend of mine came over to show me a chart he'd made. He has a great job in a corporation; he's smart, driven, by most of our standards, and has high-tech engineering skills. The graph was a plot of how much money he would have to save every year to create a pot of money that would support his lifestyle. He has expenses down to $1,000 per month—something still possible in small towns in America. By our reckoning, he has only three years to go before he can leave his job, have an income, and focus more on his love relationship and spiritual growth. He'll be out of the mainstream well before he is thirty years old. This scenario is occurring with increasing frequency among my friends. Why? Because we've finally figured out that we can't do everything—can't be everything.

What does that mean for you? That you need to set priorities. Life priorities. My mother has a life truth that I've come to believe. It goes something like this: Even though you may be good at many things and you may like to do many things, in any period of your life you can do only *two* things very well. You can build a business and be in a strong marriage. Or you can raise children and build a business. Or you can learn a new skill and be in a good marriage. The point is that some aspects of your life have to become a second priority if your business is to succeed. Not fun. Not easy. You need to choose. And I don't care what anyone else says. So, if you have decided that building your business is one of those priorities (as it should be), you get one more choice.

It is critical to know yourself and what is most important to you before you get too carried away as a business owner. If you don't know, eat some pride and get some counseling help. Priority setting is that important. If you choose, for instance, your children, then you'll need a long discussion with your mate (if you have one) about the sabbatical you need to take from the relationship. He needs to know that you love him, that you want the relationship to last, and that you can't focus on it the way you want to for the next year or so. You need to convince that person that there are many reasons why it is in his self-interest for your business to succeed (don't hesitate to mention money, vacations, better sex, a fulfilled mate, and so on). Unless you've chosen your friendships as a priority, you'll need to take some time—early on—to have the same conversation with your friends. Some may leave you. It's one of the prices of business ownership.

So set priorities. Take some quiet time to reflect on your deepest values and what *you* want from your life. Then choose the two things that will best uphold your values and help you to get whatever you said you wanted. And let the people around you know what your choices are and why. What if you have children and you choose the business and your mate? I'm simply saying here that you won't have time to personally do all the things for them that you may want to do. You won't be able to be at the soccer games and recitals. You may need to say no to the PTA and teaching Sunday school. They may be co-raised by the neighborhood teens or your parents for a while. As soon as your business kicks in (that is, you have enough sales to pay the bills and you have systems in place), you can make them a top priority again.

Believe me. Please. Many of the women I know who tried to be all things to all people are divorced, in ill-health, have kids with serious problems, and have businesses that are only stumbling along. Everyone lost because priorities weren't made. Don't make that mistake.

Once you've figured out your life priorities, than you can consider the priorities of the business. Decide what the most important activities are and figure out how to get them done. Assuming that you are working from a business plan, your priorities will probably look something like this:

- Developing a marketing strategy that makes sense for the customers.
- Selling, selling, selling.
- Paying taxes on time.
- Setting up a bookkeeping system *that is user-friendly.*
- Tracking cash flow religiously.
- Finding good people.

Write yours down and stick to them.

My Business Priorities	How They Will Get Done (Describe Process)	Who Will Be Responsible For Getting Them Done
_____	_____	_____
_____	_____	_____
_____	_____	_____
_____	_____	_____
_____	_____	_____
_____	_____	_____
_____	_____	_____

TIME MANAGEMENT: YOUR LIFE RAFT

As you look over your list, you can already see how important time management is to running a company. You need to learn how to "make time" for yourself and to "use time" effectively with the people around you. There are two parts to time management—your own personal time and how you manage it and how you spend time with other people.

Look at your personal time first. Most of us are pretty good about watching how we use up our days. We need to get better. All of us. As you move along in your business, you will discover that the only thing that slips through your hands faster than money is time. Managing it is a survival skill. There are many, many excellent books on time management as well as seminars ad nauseam. You owe yourself at least one seminar. Until then, here are some time management "tricks" that have served me well over the years:

SAYING GOOD-BYE TO CLUTTER

The first step is *getting rid of the clutter*. For some reason that I don't totally understand, the more cluttered our surroundings, the less efficient we are. (I actually use this as a screen for my professionals—a cluttered office tells me my attorney is trying to do too many things at once and won't have the time and energy to really focus on me.) You need a lot of cleared space to build your business—it creates an atmosphere conducive to efficiency. I worked with a woman last year who has a wildly successful business in that people call her from all over the country for her services, having found her through word of mouth. She contacted me because she just wasn't getting enough done in her days to make money. The first part of the problem was price. We raised hers. But the problem didn't go away. Strategic planning didn't help. A new marketing strategy, which was successful, only made the problem worse. It finally occurred to me that her office—cozy, picture-filled, souvenir-crammed, and cluttered from floor to ceiling—might be part of the problem. She got the homework assignment of cleaning out half the clutter and—miracle of miracles—her efficiency improved dramatically. So we took the plunge and got rid of everything that was unnecessary to her work except for her special tea cup and one family picture and voilà—she is a woman to be reckoned with. She bought a huge desk, more bookcases for industry reference material, doubled her filing cabinets, and she was on her way.

Get rid of the clutter. Thank your children for the school art and stash it in a drawer somewhere. Give your trophies away. Take a Polaroid picture of them for the memory if you need to—then give them away.

When you are done, you can take what's left and organize it into priority order. I literally sort all my tasks according to when they need to be done and put everything into one pile, with the most important task on the top. Then I simply work my way through the pile. I used to keep the pile right on my desk, but there are some days when it's so high that it stops me dead. So I keep it behind me and use the desk to work on the top task.

If I have activities that need to be done at a later date, I simply store them in an accordion folder marked by dates—I can then organize months at a time when I get to them. For example, if I need to start organizing Deloitte & Touche's entrepreneurial seminar series in January and it is now October, I write myself a reminder note and put it into the January section of the folder. That way I don't work on something until I need to and I don't have it hanging over my head prematurely.

I also try to touch any paper *once*. When I get mail, I skim it and either:

a. Toss it.

b. Set it aside with a note to myself regarding what I need to do to get it off my desk.

or

c. Put a note on it to someone else so they can take care of it.

My goal is to get everything to fall into (a) or (c). What does that mean? Well, one of the things it means is that I don't take time to read all the journals that come through; instead, I flip through them and rip out the articles I really want to read or, if that sounds too barbarian for your tastes, mark the articles I want photocopied so I can recycle the magazine. The result: no piles of newspapers and magazines that aren't getting read and that create guilt in me every time I notice the pile! A related trick: Don't keep copies of anything you know someone else will be keeping, unless of course you need it right now. You'll save trees and get rid of even more clutter.

On dealing with mail. First off, as a business owner you are no longer obligated to answer every piece of mail you receive. So throw away as much as you can.

If you get a letter that you can respond to with a couple of sentences, reply right then and there. Pick up the phone and call or jot a note right on the letter. Or type a response right out on the computer. Over the years, I've found that a lot of correspondence I receive is similar so I've developed form letters and memos that I can change slightly to serve as a response.

Edwin S. Bliss, in *Getting Things Done,* offers many time-saving techniques related to mail. My favorite is where he tells the reader not to waste time on flowery language or big words. Instead, just say what you have to say and be done with it. He also suggests that you don't write when a phone call will do.

Give yourself the gift of *uninterrupted time.* It can be the first hour of your day. Or the last hour. A lunch hour. You want time free from phone calls, visitors, mail, things to read. Unplug the phone if you have to. Lock your door. Put a sign on it that warns people of the consequences of entering. Do what you have to and watch the results. One hour of uninterrupted time can double a person's productivity for the day. This is especially true if you use it to organize a "to do" list and outline a time line and task list for more complicated chores.

Which brings me to "to do" lists. If you don't use them, you'll fail. Why? Because too much will fall through the cracks. I start every day with a "to do" list, and I rank every job in order of priority and check each off as I go along. Sometimes I'll even write in a reward on the list. For example, I've been known to give myself the gift of a walk down Main Street as a reward for completing a difficult project. Anything I don't complete by the end of the day is automatically written down on the next day's list—before I go home. That way everything gets done eventually. I also put deadlines on anything I carry forward to ensure that I don't carry the task forward into infinity.

And do one thing at a time. There is always a temptation to sort mail while you are on the phone or work on a different task when you are in a meeting. Everyone suffers as a result. People know when you aren't really listening to them (don't you?) and I can't tell you how many times I used to miss important points in a meeting because I was busy trying to get something else done at the same time. Do one thing at a time. If the meeting is a waste of time, change it or leave. You aren't obligated to hear all the trials and tribulations of your banker's labor pains. Just tell her you appreciate how difficult it must have been and when you have more time it might be fun to compare notes, but right now you have some deadlines to meet. Everyone understands deadlines, and as a business owner every day is fraught with deadlines. Let people know! Remind them. They'll understand. The ones who don't will fall by the wayside anyway, because sooner or later you'll make them mad because of your "lack of consideration." Oh well. Let them go. *You don't have time to people please—you have a business to run.*

CONFERENCE CALLS

Three years ago, I added up all the hours I spend needlessly driving to meetings that could have been done in the form of a conference call. I lost over 200 hours in the course of a year.

I am not saying that every meeting can be a conference call. First-time meetings, project-organizing meetings, key negotiation sessions, wrap-up meetings, and birthday parties are all ill-suited to conference calls. I know. I tried. On the other hand, team updates, staff meetings when staff are scattered geographically, budget meetings, and many client meetings can be done and done well over the telephone. All you have to do is call the operator and give him or her a list of the names and telephone numbers of everyone participating and she'll take it from there. Or you can probably use your own telephone system if it has any sophistication at all.

Don't limit conference calls to business. You can have executive-committee meetings for your church board, organize the PTA's fund-raising, and coordinate the family's Christmas brunch via telephone.

MINIMIZING INTERRUPTIONS

Interruptions are an integral part of the life of any business owner. In fact, you should want interruptions. You should want customers to call and employees to double check with you if they are unsure about a certain procedure. Having said that—there are two ways to lessen the number of interruptions in a day. One that I like a lot is to make all my telephone calls at once instead of throughout the day. As a business owner, you can expect anywhere from twenty to fifty phone calls a day depending on the type of enterprise. I've learned that by returning my phone calls between 11:00 A.M. and noon and 4:00 and 5:00 P.M. I can keep them short and to the point because people are either hungry and starting to think about lunch or they are trying to gear down at the end of the day.

Although I personally answer my line whenever I'm in the office, on deadline days I ask my assistant not only to accept all calls, I also ask her to see if she can help whoever it is.

WHY BUSINESS LUNCHES ARE A LOUSY IDEA

I dislike business lunches. They always last two hours when you have only one. Of that time, business usually takes up all of fifteen to twenty minutes, while socializing takes up an hour or more. If I'm with a man, the socializing part can get uncomfortable (what can we talk about?!). Sports uses up only five to ten minutes. Politics is dangerous. So is religion. He won't want to talk about his relationships, and I know nothing about cars, hunting, fishing, or Rush Limbaugh. Don't get me wrong. I think socializing is swell—but not in the middle of my day when there is already too much to do. Plus, you'll often feel obligated to pay, which gets expensive. And you'll eat more than you mean to because you are sitting there thinking about all the things you aren't getting done. And then, if you leave before the other person is ready to end the meeting, he or she will be irritated.

You can't win. I say it's better to save your money, calories, and time and go for that walk or take a break and sit in a cafe for a half hour with a good book. Or grocery shop. You will be amazed at how many errands you can run in a lunch hour when you set your mind to it. Plus, you get a break from the office, which gives your brain a rest and can get your creative juices going again. If you have real courage, lock your door and take a nap. One of the most wonderful speeches I heard this year was by a newly instated president of a Midwestern university. In his inaugural speech, he announced his strong support for naps. To his mind, all civilized countries but ours have learned the business, social, and psychological benefits of naps and it was time we tried it out. I agree. Try it. You'll be stunned at how effective and efficient your afternoon becomes.

RUNNING EFFICIENT MEETINGS

There are key ground rules to running great short meetings. Follow them and you will be one happy camper:

- Send out an agenda beforehand. Not just any agenda, mind you. This agenda should list topics to be discussed, who is responsible for running the discussion, how long the topic is allotted, what decisions, if any, need to be made, and your preliminary thoughts about the decisions—if you have any.
- Start on time. Don't wait for stragglers. They'll learn.
- Follow the agenda to the minute.
- Assign follow-up tasks at the meeting.
- End on time. Every time. So your staff know they can trust you to do what you say you will do, when you say you will.
- Follow up with a reminder memo that reminds everyone what they need to do.

PROCRASTINATION

Don't do it. Don't let yourself. Procrastination wastes whole days. It quickly leads to failed businesses if you procrastinate on the wrong things, like paying taxes. You need to do the tasks on your "to do" list when you've told yourself you would. If you find that procrastination is something that haunts you incessantly, figure out why. Get a good therapist to help. My male friends tell me procrastination comes from being afraid that you'll make a mistake. While that may be true, I've also noticed that a lot of women procrastinate in a way that sabotages their success. They aren't afraid of being wrong—they're afraid of being right!

Part of why we procrastinate can also be because we've agreed to do things we simply don't want to do. Think of all the things you've volunteered to do in your life. Did they come last (assuming they got done)? As a business owner, you will find that agreeing to too many things stops you cold. Nothing gets done because you lose track of activities, or forget where you were going to start, or just plain don't have the energy to do what you promised to do. What is the solution? *Just say no.* Say no to anything you don't feel morally or economically bound to do. You cannot build a business if you try to be too many things to too many people. One of the best ways to give yourself the gift of time is to gracefully decline the request. Since, as a woman, I know this is easier said than done, here's how I say no. I always repeat back the request so the person knows I've heard. Then, if I have another activity planned, I have an obvious excuse. But what if I don't, what if I just need to be in the office? Then my response is that I can't because I have another obligation (that is, *to be in the office*). For entrepreneurs, that is reason enough.

Once your business has taken on a successful life of its own, then you will be able to say yes to more things. (Not that you'll want to. But it won't matter then because you'll be much better at simply saying no—without explanation.)

TIME MANAGEMENT AND OTHER PEOPLE

Aim for clarity at all times in all places. You know yourself how much time is wasted when we circle a topic instead of coming right out and talking about it. Indirectness cost me years in a marriage. It is costing you right now. Forget Amy Vanderbilt and all those rules your aunts and grandmother taught you about finding something nice to say. *You don't have time.* If something is wrong, say it. Define it. Outline steps to fix it.

This is not a call for bitchiness. I never aim at the person. So, if you feel an uncontrollable urge to tell someone that he or she is the most incredibly stupid person ever to defile the face of the earth and you rue the day he or she dropped into your life—go take a walk. And keep walking until you are able to focus on the thing, on *what* is bothering you and not the person.

Challenge sloppy work. Late work. Poor attitude. They all cost time. Listen. Really listen to the people you are working with. Listen sympathetically. Be able to say back what they said to you. Knowing where your staff is coming from saves time. Show concern for their well being. This is not the same thing as being a surrogate mother; it's more like showing what Buddhists call "loving kindness." Remember, happy employees are efficient employees.

DELEGATION

Moses had to do it. Kings have to do it. So do presidents and movie stars and television anchor women. All business owners need to learn how to do it. Remember, you are not omnipotent—no one is. To build your company, you'll have to share, because as John Keats would have said if he were alive today, "No woman is an island." You will exhaust yourself trying to do everything. You don't have time anyway.

There are two phases to delegating. In the first phase, you teach your team the lay of the land: what your values are, your goals for the business, to whom you sell, financial operations, and how things are done. In the second phase, you let go. You can delegate your tasks to your staff, starting with small and routine matters and building (if you're smart) to virtually everything you do.

What is delegation? I offer you a definition from Dale Mc-Conkey in his book *No-Nonsense Delegation:*

1. The determination of priorities.

2. The translation of the priorities into objectives or results for the organizational unit.

3. The breaking down of the organizational objectives into smaller units to be clearly delegated to managers.

4. The establishment of a feedback system to monitor the effectiveness of the delegation.

You need to empower and motivate. How? By teaching staff what you do and why you do it. Where do you start? By picking the right person, a person who wants to succeed, a person who listens, a person who knows how to make decisions. It's to be hoped that you are thinking of who it is as you read this. If you are having a difficult time deciding if the staff you have hired (or are about to hire) fits the bill, you may have hired the wrong person. Step one is making sure you have access to the right person. The second step is to approach the person about the task, describe the opportunity, and ask for feedback. You want to make sure you have a match before you waste time for both of you. Once you have a sense that the person understands the task and wants to try it out, you can get started. Delegate gradually. Give that person one new task at a time. Have her watch how you do it, then have her do it with you, and then have her try it herself and show you the results. If they are what you were after, you are home free—delegate away. If not, go over the process again until she gets it. If she's the right person, she will— sooner or later. Give her room to make mistakes. Leave her alone to practice at her own pace. Add the new task to her job description so you can keep track of everything she's doing— and reward her generously when she has the task down. She has just given you back some valuable time.

The best delegators actually write out a sort of instruction manual when they delegate tasks. They also take time to let other team members know what is going on. They make sure to keep any necessary information flowing to the "delegatee," which will help her do a better job. And they absolutely transfer the *authority for the task* to the subordinate. You need the courage to leave her alone to carry out the assignment. Watch yourself on this one. Most business owners sooner or later figure out how to share responsibility. Fewer learn how to share authority (that is, the power to move resources to where they are needed).

To delegate well, you need to peel your fingers off your need to keep all the authority in your pocket.

Once you get the hang of delegation, you'll love it. It will free your time and lead to creative ideas related to better performing the functions of the business (because two heads really are better than one). It will define you as someone people want to work for—someone who, while focused on results, has the self-esteem she needs to allow subordinates to play with the methods.

I am not saying that you are handing over total freedom. You want some mutually agreed-upon checkpoints that will prevent any serious catastrophes as your staff feels her way. When problems do arise, and they will, ask for your staff's recommendation. In my experience, they always have an excellent idea regarding how the problem can be solved.

Take the time. Start with in-house operations and move out to sales, marketing, and, finally, financial jobs.

Before you take the plunge, I want to review the biggest delegation mistakes I've seen women business owners make so you'll know better:

1. *Not being clear.* Most women business owners are always moving fast. You've a lot of balls to juggle. You *cannot* assume that just because you've explained the task your staff has any idea what you said. Usually they don't because we tend to give them the first and last sentences of what we want, completely skipping the middle!

2. *Failing to give staff the authority to perform their jobs.* Allow them to make the decisions they need to make to succeed.

3. *Getting caught up in procedures instead of objectives.* Why should you care how something gets done as long as the process was legal and ethical? Be more concerned with *if* it gets done. Focus on objectives, not procedures.

4. *Assigning tasks instead of delegating them.* We all have things we want to delegate to someone else because we hate doing them. Passing on a task you hate doing isn't delegating, it's *assigning*. It's the same thing as saying, "I'm higher than you so you have to do this awful chore." While every manager does some assigning (since we *are* all human), too much assigning leads to recriminations and resignations. Staff hate it. Instead, delegate what is appropriate. Delegate what you can appropriately delegate—the jobs people *want* to learn. Jobs where staff do gain in responsibility and authority. Jobs where staff learn how to be better staff.

5. *Perfectionism.* Here is why perfectionists work and live alone in the end. Because we're not perfect. Not a one of us. Wanting everything to be perfect is neurotic. It frustrates everyone to the point of fury. It sets you, and everyone around you, up for failure. Sooner or later, the sane people around you will leave. Aim for excellence instead.

6. *Failing to give credit to the employee for a job well done.* You know better. Something like half of all women who start their own businesses do so because they are tired of doing their boss's job and never getting any credit for it. Stop the pattern. *Give your staff credit wherever and whenever you can.* Privately. Publicly. Repeatedly.

7. *Giving staff too much to do.* You may be willing to work sixty hours a week for no pay, but your staff isn't. What they want to do is give you a fair day's work for a fair day's pay. If you overburden them, they'll leave. Signs include consistently missed deadlines, sloppy work, or half-done projects. Or they'll keep trying to interrupt you for guidance and you'll never quite get around to stopping what you are doing to help them.

LARKIN'S OWN LOOPING BACK SYSTEM

Use this whenever you delegate a task:

Task Assigned	Person Assigned	Date It Was Supposed to Be Completed	How I Know It Was Done

---

STEP-BY-STEP DELEGATION CHART

1. Determine what to delegate.
2. Determine to whom to delegate.
3. Discuss the overall results expected.
4. Agree on the specific results expected.
5. Agree on the time period.
6. Agree on the authority and resources.
7. Establish controls and reporting.
8. Double-check for understanding.
9. Continually evaluate performance.
10. Recognize and reward the delegatee.
11. Coach and counsel for improvement.

A LAST WORD ON MANAGING YOUR BUSINESS

Everyone you work with will want to know everything about you. And with good reason. You are an interesting and exciting woman. A risk taker. A decision maker. A problem solver. One of the worst things you can do is bring your personal life into the business. It give your staff an excuse to waste time (talking about your latest life experience). And if they start evaluating how you run your personal life (And they will. And you already know that you won't get high marks because you are putting everything you have into your business so your personal life is bound to suffer!), those evaluations will start to impact their perceptions of you as a manager. Keep your personal life to yourself. If you need someone as a sounding board, go to a friend. If you have no friends—which is possible since you've isolated yourself to build this company—find a counselor or a support group. Never, ever use employees for emotional sounding boards. You'll regret it. Over and over again. Especially if you ever face firing one of them.

CHAPTER 9

MARKETING

TRUTHS

Whenever I get to a fork in the road I choose it.
Yogi Berra

Forget the act of selling for now. Before you advertise, telephone clients, or start any door-to-dooring, you need to do some strategic thinking about marketing. I've discovered, over the years, that most women who start their own businesses start with a strong intuitive sense of what product they want to sell and who they believe the customers will be. Once the company kicks in, however, problems begin. Part of the reason is that there is just too much on your plate for you to sit quietly and think about your product, let alone your customers. Part of the reason is that the more involved you are in the operations of your business the farther you are from the street, which means you are no longer getting data about the world to egg your intuition into gear.

What to do? Well, the first thing to know is that in marketing it's okay to start with your intuition (that is, your gut feeling regarding products and markets). Once you've identified your product, you need to face one of those moments of truth. It goes something like this: You need to ask yourself if you have identified a product that is a solution to a problem. An example is the van service available to my ten-year-old to truck her to ballet class and soccer practice

177

after school when I'm out of town. The van service is solving a huge problem for working parents or parents who may not have access to transportation during the day.

If you are sure you have a product that solves a problem, your next question needs to be: Who has that problem? Again, use your intuition. Who do you think has the problem—whether they know it or not? And, finally, how do you think you'll get their attention so you can sell your product?

Once you have your intuitive answers to these questions, you are ready to do some real market research.

When it comes to getting customers, the 1990s are making the 1980s look like child's play. We each have something like a million pieces of information coming at us every day. As a result, we're screening out more and more. We "mute" our television sets for the commercials. We stick Walkmen in our ears so we don't notice the noise on the street. We skim our newspapers and use speaker phones so we can sort our mail or do some other paperwork while we're talking on the phone. What that means for every woman business owner is that you need to track the goings-on of the world so you can keep your finger on your customers' pulses. Because if you don't, someone else will.

AN ENVIRONMENTAL ANALYSIS

How? First by doing something called an environmental analysis. In the jargon of the industry, this is simply a look at the world around you to see what *trends* are out there. You want to focus on four kinds of trends: economic, legal/political, people, and technological. They each impact our values, what we buy and how we buy. The economic environment is basically a summary of the total business climate for where you want to sell your product. Is the economy strong? Is it getting better? Do people have money to spend? Are they spending it? What about unemployment—is it growing? How about inflation? The number of new businesses? Business failures?

Legal and political questions have more to do with whether you'll have a lot of regulations in your face or the freedom to design what you really think the market wants. It has to do with how stable the political system is where you are planning to sell. Think about liability. Whether we like it or not, we live in a lawsuit feeding-frenzy culture. Beware. Figure out how susceptible you are to legal problems *before* you start formally designing the product. Every year two or three companies I know go out of business because they simply cannot afford the cost of liability insurance. Usually, they are making a children's product. Often it is a plastic toy.

People questions are demographics: our ages, our racial makeup, our incomes, lifestyles, and values. There are lots and lots of people trends. You need to discover them and think about their impact on your product choice and how you sell. For example, we're all getting older by the minute. The fastest-growing population group in the United States— right now—is the elderly. Perhaps your lettering should be bigger, your ingredients should be explained more completely, and so forth. In the United States, we're also increasingly multicultural and multiethnic. What does that mean for you? The middle class is disappearing, so you don't want to aim a product in that direction. We care more and more about spiritual things, and everybody is worried about Mother Earth and whether we've become too large a bacteria for her to survive us.

Technological trends will also impact you. Think about what is going on there. Given all the scientists out there, major breakthroughs can be expected. They will make technology smaller (the Dick Tracy watch is here!), cheaper, and stronger by the minute. Don't position yourself to sell a technology unless you are personally related to Bill Gates and have a full-time espionage team watching your potential competitors. There's just too much technology-shifting going on for you to take a chance.

How to track all these goings-on? Two ways—through people and through written material. Let me start with people. To my mind, Faith Popcorn has perfected the technique of creating a think tank. You owe it to yourself to pick up a copy of *The Popcorn Report* and to see what trends she sees for the future and to understand how she uses think tanks.

THINK TANK EQUIVALENTS

Okay, so you can't collect 2,000 of the most creative thinkers in the industry to help you predict the future. And you can't afford to do the 3,000 nationwide surveys Faith does every year. What can you do? Lots of things. Start a salon. Salons started back in a quieter, slower time (the eighteenth century, I think) when groups of smart, creative people would gather regularly at someone's house (often a famous artist) to discuss the trends of the day. What new things were happening? How were people reacting? What were the implications of these trends?

You can do the same thing. Start making a list of ten to twelve of the most creative people you know. The more diverse the group the better. Find a researcher, a scientist, a nurse, a money manager, an artist, a geek, a computer lover, a reporter, a physician, the oldest person you know, a precocious eleven-year-old, a teenager, someone in her twenties. Mix up races. And sex. And lifestyle. Invite them to brunch. Feed them well and ask them what is going on politically, economically, in technology, and related to people. Listen to them. Then ask them what they think all these trends mean for you. Listen some more. Then thank them. Give them presents. Invite them back in a month or two. Let them be your window on the world. You will thank me forever and ever because they will help you with your marketing more than any other single thing you can do.

You can use your customers or potential customers as a resource bank as well. Take a group of four to six customers to lunch on a regular basis. Ask them about your product idea. What do they like? What don't they like? What else do they want? How do they want you to sell to them?

At worst, you owe it to yourself to do periodic mail surveys of customers or potential customers. At a minimum, it will tell them you are interested in them. At best, a mail survey will give you terrific insights into your customer base. I don't know what it is about entrepreneurs that keeps us from asking for feedback. It must be that we don't want to hear anything negative because it will cost us money to change whatever received the low marks. All I know is that customer feedback is priceless. Make it your friend. Don't let it become that last task on your to-do list that never quite gets done.

You can develop your own survey. It doesn't even need a lot of questions. Here's how to increase your chances of getting responses:

1. Give the respondent something. A copy of your company newsletter if you have one. A dollar. A sprig of mistletoe in the holiday season. A cartoon on a magnet. Some stamps. Some stickers. A small (thin) gift that fits into an envelope and isn't too schmaltzy helps your response rate. The more unusual the better. (Everybody has tried those preprinted return-address labels and pencils. Go for something more related to your business.)

2. Write a *personal note* (no form letters allowed!) to the person from whom you need the response and tell her exactly what you are trying to do. I really mean a personal note. In your handwriting. You can write bunches while you watch that television show you love but that's politically incorrect to watch because it's pure trash. That said television show is a perfect backdrop for writing the same note over and over—it will keep you mildly entertained while you significantly increase your chances of getting feedback. What do you say in the letter? The truth.

Here's an example to get your creative juices started. The best letter should be in your own words. If you didn't happen to major in English composition in college, you might consider getting a writer friend to take a look at your draft to tighten it and correct any spelling errors before you begin your personal-letter assembly-line writing night. (Yes, you can pay your teenage daughter to help you write that night. Her handwriting should be vaguely like yours and still be feminine enough to be attractive. Forget husbands, sons, and anyone under ten or over seventy—as a general rule. Just make sure you sign the letter to keep your credibility intact.)

Write the letter on your letterhead and resist the temptation to put labels on the envelopes. How often do you open a letter with a label on it? Everybody I know throws them out because we don't have time to read real letters, let alone "junk mail." And put a pretty stamp on the letter. It not only cheers up the recipient, it may end up as an extra gift if she is a stamp collector.

Always, always include a self-addressed, *stamped* envelope so they can easily send their responses back to you.

Now, for a sample letter. Let me say, again, that your own words will work best. If you don't know where to start, this might help:

SAMPLE SURVEY COVER LETTER

Earth Love Laces
101 North Main
Ann Arbor, MI 48104
313-737-5555

February 14, 1993

Dear Ms. Snarley, [Make sure to use their names. Dear customer or anything that impersonal guarantees a toss to the garbage can.]

For ten years my sister and I have been making hand-made lace products out of silk produced by the Women's Co-op in Costa Rica. Although many of our friends have urged us to sell the lace commercially, we have hesitated up until now. Recently, however, we decided to open a business together and need your feedback regarding whether our primary product should be lace. As you are a subscriber of *Rural America* magazine, we believe that you represent our customer. [You know this because you bought a list of the subscribers to the magazine in your geographical market at a dollar a name.]

I have enclosed a handkerchief representing our handwork as a thank-you for taking a couple of minutes to answer the enclosed questionnaire. You'll also see that a self-addressed, stamped envelope has been enclosed for your convenience.

Thank you. If we get sufficient positive feedback, we plan to start a monthly ad campaign selling our products in *Rural America* beginning in May. Please watch for us. Thank you again.

Sincerely,

(You)
President

The main points of the letter are:

1. Why you are writing.
2. What you are selling.
3. How they can help (that is, by filling out the survey and sending it back to you).

Surveys sound scarier than they really are. You've filled out enough surveys to know what they should look like. If not, watch your mail for the next couple of months. Someone is sure to send you one.

A couple of truths about surveys:

1. The shorter they are the better. If a survey looks too long, *no one* will answer it. Too long these days is more than two sides of a page or about 20 to 25 questions.

2. The easier they are to answer, the better. Try to ask questions that can be answered yes or no or with one or two words. In the language of survey research, these are called closed-ended questions.

An example survey might look like this:

1. Do you own lace?   ❑ YES ❑ NO
2. Please check the types of lace product you own:
   ☐ Tablecloth
   ☐ Napkins
   ☐ Handkerchief
   ☐ Doilies for furniture
   ☐ Lingerie
   ☐ Baby garments
   ☐ Gloves
   ☐ Stockings
   ☐ Other (please list here _____)

3. Please list a price you might expect to pay for each of these items:

4. Do you purchase lace? ❑ YES ❑ NO
   - ☐ Tablecloth
   - ☐ Napkins
   - ☐ Handkerchief
   - ☐ Doilies for furniture
   - ☐ Lingerie
   - ☐ Baby garments
   - ☐ Gloves
   - ☐ Stockings
   - ☐ Other (please list here _____
     _____)

   If you answered no, please skip to question 7.

5. Where do you purchase it?
   - ☐ Catalogue (please name the catalogue _____)
   - ☐ Store near you (please name the store _____)
   - ☐ Craft fairs (please name which fair(s) _____)

6. How often do you purchase a lace product?
   - ☐ Less than once per month
   - ☐ Once per month
   - ☐ Several times a year
   - ☐ Annually
   - ☐ Once every few years
   - ☐ Other _____

7. Please tell us a little about you:

   What is your sex? ☐ Male ☐ Female

What is your age?

☐ Over 65
☐ 61-65
☐ 51-60
☐ 35-50
☐ 22-34
☐ 13-21

What is your income level?

☐ Under $5,000
☐ $5,000-$9,999
☐ $10,000-$14,999
☐ $15,000-$29,999
☐ $30,000-$49,999
☐ $50,000-$69,999
☐ $70,000-$99,999
☐ $100,000 or over

What is your educational level?

☐ Some high school
☐ Some college
☐ Associate's degree
☐ Bachelor's degree
☐ Some graduate school
☐ Advanced degree

What is your profession?

☐ Homemaker
☐ Student
☐ Self-employed
☐ Service
☐ Retail
☐ Manufacturing

Please add any additional comments here:

_____

_____

If you know anyone who knows anything about survey research, ask them to take a look at your survey before you mail it to anyone. If you don't know someone (and even if you do), try the questionnaire out on a couple of people who would be customers if your business were up and running, or are already customers if you are in business, and ask for their feedback. Should you have more questions? If yes, what should they be? Fewer? Did they understand the questions? Were they offended by any of them? Take their suggestions, make your changes, and mail away. Keep mailing surveys until you get at least a hundred back, so you can see patterns of response.

Then do the same thing next year. And the year after that. And the year after that . . . until you sell the business to go play.

LIBRARIES

You can trust a crystal ball about as far as you can throw it.
Faith Popcorn

Libraries are the most underrespected institutions in America. I could spend my whole life in a library. Just about everything you need to know about markets can be tracked down by a good librarian. If she doesn't have it there, she'll tell you whom to call or where to write for more specific help. And now every self-respecting library offers computers where you can do database searches of hundreds of *thousands* of journals, books, and other documents to help you get information about your market, market trends, and customers.

On the chance that you'll gasp helplessly the first time you walk into a library to start your research, here is a list of my all-time favorite sources of information for the market research I do for clients:

First the databases. Call me old-fashioned, but I learned on Dialog so that's what I use. It has more than 200 of its own databases, which include industry reports, the major journals and newspapers, scientific studies, and even speeches by company presidents.

Then there are the economic reports. I have learned to deeply appreciate the researchers at the U.S. Department of Commerce. Their Business Conditions Digest is an excellent and fair summary of many of the economic indicators. Dun & Bradstreet's industry reports are also chockfull of market data that will be useful to you. Other sources of economic material range from *Fortune* magazine and *Inc.* to *Business Week, The Wall Street Journal,* and, if you have time, the Sunday *New York Times Week in Review Section.* (When you just have to punt because you have no time, stick with *Fortune* and *Inc.* They've kept me covered for years.)

Libraries will have future trend information, including the "Kiplinger Washington Letter" and John Naisbitt's trend report. Don't go back too far—a couple of issues will do. They will also have lists upon lists of names of associations and government agencies that can help you to identify legal trends (that is, regulations) that are coming your way. Don't allow yourself to be surprised by legal or political trends. Find out what is going on so you can turn it into a marketing advantage. As an example of how critical this is, I watched a construction company track the American Disabilities Act as it made its way through Congress, and when everyone else in the industry was hanging onto existing markets this company started to sell itself as an expert in American Disabilities Act compliance for small companies. They had identified all the building changes called for in the act, made deals with all the suppliers they needed, and today their telephone is ringing off the hook. That's the power of tracking written information.

Allow yourself to roam in the library. Check out the Yellow Pages where you plan to sell your product. See who else is out there. Get on association mailing lists. Get trade-show information even if you aren't planning to go to the show. You'll still get an idea of what is hot in your market.

In *Twelve Simple Steps to a Winning Marketing Plan* (Probus, 1992), I spend a chapter talking about the reader through something called a five-step marathon, which has as its goal helping you to figure out what is triggering consumers' interests these days. In oversimplified form, the steps include going to shopping malls to let your senses key in on what people are attracted to, doing library research, skimming a wide variety of magazines to see what people care about, watching television commercials to see what advertisers think we want in our lives, and knowing a little about the books that are making it to *The New York Times* best-seller list. The whole point of the exercise is to allow your subconscious or intuitive side to take over. You overexpose yourself to information and then let your subconscious take over and tell you what patterns and themes are out there. Why are they important? Because knowing them will help you to get your customers' attention. For example, if the colors we're all seeing are bright, clear colors, you don't want brochures in subtle hues—soft grays, mauves—because they'll be lost in the crowd. Any crowd.

I last did the five-step marathon prior to the 1992 presidential race. Three patterns emerged. One was what I'd call a "protect Mother Earth" pattern where there was a lot of softness, efficiency, almost austerity (because the less we have to use, the easier we are on the earth). A second theme can only be called a "slut" theme. Just when I'd be saying to myself, time to give up my polyester pants and go for the soft cottonwear or use-it-forever products, I'd stumble into a section of a store filled with short (as in barely covering the buttocks) skirted black velvet dresses with sequins or tassels at the nipples or something equally slutlike. I couldn't figure it out at first, so I let my intuition take over and here's what I came up with: We are all trying to be good kids. We eat our vegetables, recycle, buy cotton and wool clothes, volunteer at food banks, and spend more and more time at home for our "leisure." But, every once in awhile, say once every six to eight weeks, we just need to let loose, to play, to disco, to wear Victoria's Secret panties.

As soon as I understood the dimensions, I realized that there were all sorts of marketing implications. Are you selling your product to someone on a "good kid" day or on a "let it out" day? It matters. I've watched a woman target the slut theme to great success. She rents expensive trampy dresses with price tags of $1,500 to $3,000 for $100 to $200, and she can't keep her wares in stock. At the other end, a friend of mine is capitalizing on the protect-mother earth trend. She opened a retail store, Terra Bella, which carries only earth-friendly products. The store has its own waterfall, palm trees, and crowds of customers. Her intuition told her that our concern for the environment will only get stronger and be reflected in consumer behavior. Time is proving her right.

The third theme can only be called Americana—red, white, and blue in the form of stars, stripes, and dots was everywhere. If products were made in the USA, they were labelled as such, openly and proudly. That told me that baseball caps would be a fail-safe gift for clients—particularly ones made of cotton, in red, white, or blue and with your logo on it.

Try the marathon. You'll have fun and be astounded at how clearly you will see patterns and tastes that you can work into your own sales efforts.

FIND THE ANGLE

As you observe everything, you want to keep a special eye out for competitive products and the companies who sell them. You have competition. Women tend not to want to admit this. I think it reminds us of our painful high school years when we never quite timed a crush on some football hero when we could lust after him on our own. There was always someone else after him too and usually they were in our own friendship circle. So, we pretended that we weren't competitors. Well, we were wrong then, and we're wrong if we have the same mindset now. There is always competition. The sooner you figure out who your competitors are and how they are competing with you, the better off you'll be. One of the best business ideas I ever heard, as the mother of a precocious ten-year-old, was for a "Motel 6" for kids where parents who worked jobs from other than 8:00 A.M. to 5:00 P.M. could leave their children, including overnight. The woman who put the business plan together was a very successful businesswoman, worth millions in her own right, who needed a significant amount of capital to either build a chain or renovate existing buildings for the business. Venture capitalists turned the deal down cold. The reason was her competition. Even though her idea was unique in that there were no other comparable kid-hotels out there, she just couldn't stand up to the competition—teenagers, other relatives, or simply leaving the children on their own.

So figure out who is your competition. It is the people or companies who are now providing the function you provide. I write business plans and initial market strategies for my clients. The people and companies who would be performing those tasks if it weren't for me range from other management consultants at international firms such as Deloitte & Touche, to other management consultants at regional or local firms, to graduate students, to marketing and strategic-planning professionals in between jobs, to retired professionals who provide free counseling, to entrepreneurs through the good graces of the Small Business Administration.

Always, always, always think about the strengths and weaknesses of your competition. As you do, gaps should emerge. For example, when I analyzed my competition, I found only two other women who did what I do in the Ann Arbor area. Although they are both excellent service professionals, neither does very well *transferring their skill sets to their clients*. That is the gap I decided to fill. Not only would I write business plans, but I would teach my clients to write their own so they wouldn't need me anymore (I figure there are plenty of you out there!). That's my angle. That's what is special about me. I do it *and* I teach it—through seminars, books, and one-on-one counseling sessions. That's my market position.

You need an angle. Something unique about you. Try using the following chart to figure out what it is:

MY COMPETITION IS:

Name of competitors (this can be generic as in "management consultants from other big firms"):

1.

2.

3.

4.

5.

The strengths of each of these competitors are:

Strengths

Competitor #1: _____

_____

_____

_____

Strengths

Competitor #2: _____
_____
_____
_____

Competitor #3: _____
_____
_____
_____

Competitor #4: _____
_____
_____
_____

Competitor #5: _____
_____
_____
_____

Their weaknesses are:

Weaknesses

Competitor #1: _____
_____
_____
_____

Competitor #2: _____
_____
_____
_____

Competitor #3: _____
_____
_____
_____

Competitor #4: _____
_____
_____
_____

Competitor #5: _____
_____
_____
_____

Looking at my competitors, here are the gaps:
_____
_____
_____
_____

Therefore, my "angle" or market position is:
_____
_____
_____
_____

Once you figure out your angle, decide to be the best, since you really have no choice. Consumers increasingly demand quality of all of us. Give it to them before they ask. Be the best. If you can be only that one thing. If you can be only the best for a small market, then aim for being a big fish in your own small pond.

On Being a Big Fish in Your Own Pond

This one might be counterintuitive to you. (Really it isn't, but it might seem as if it is at first.) The biggest mistake many women make is trying to be too many things to too many people—we try to be a big fish in a big pond. Wrong. Think about your market (that is, all the people or companies who need your product). Then take that group and separate out the ones who want your product. You'll notice that it's a much smaller group. If you aren't sure who wants your product, keep asking people who need your product until a profile of those who want it emerges. For example, even though all business owners need my products, I've found out that a particular type of owner wants my services and is willing to pay for it. Then, you need to ask yourself: Of this second group, who will pay for my product? Her profile looks like this:

- Business owner
- Based in lower peninsula of Michigan
- Within sixty-minute drive of Ann Arbor
- Female
- Thirty to fifty years old
- A decision maker
- Trusts other women
- Has an income
- Has owned business less than three to five years
- Had experience running a business before
- Knows how to use consultants (that is, has used consultants before)
- Capable of delegating
- Has an accountant
- Has an attorney
- Has at least one employee
- Has strong opinions
- Wants to grow the company to a size where she'll be financially well off (that is, wants income of better than $150,000 a year)
- Married
- At least one of her parents was an entrepreneur or in sales

As you can see, this is a small group, relative to all the business owners out there.

You want to do the same thing. First, define all the people or companies out there who need your product:

If you sell to companies:

Where are they located (nationally, in certain states, within sixty miles of your home) _____

How old should the company be? _____

How many employees does it have? _____

What do its revenues need to be? _____

Does it need to be profitable to buy your product? _____

If the answer is yes, how profitable? _____

Does it need to be in a particular industry? _____

If yes, what industry(ies)? _____

What should its products lines be? _____

Does it need to be a certain style (such as risk taking or risk acceptant or conservative)? _____

If yes, what style? _____

Does it need to have a particular buying behavior (such as the president needing to approve the purchase)? _____

If yes, what is the buying behavior needed? _____

If you are selling to people, you need to define these characteristics:

Where they live geographically _____

The type of community they live in (rural, urban, suburban, etc.) _____

Sex _____

Race _____

Income level _____

Marital status _____

Whether they are parents _____

Level of education _____

Political inclinations _____

Type of employment _____

Any particular buying behavior (that is, they need to be able to use a VISA card) _____

Now look at your list and ask yourself the following question: Of all those people I've just defined, who really wants my product? Add any information to your profile that will help you to weed out the wrong customers. Now ask yourself who will actually pay for the product. You should end up with a profile that is at least as specific as mine. It's a small pond—but you'll be the big fish, and that's what will bring you business success.

PUBLIC RELATIONS

We always forget this part. Or give it too low a priority. I think it's because we all hate writing press releases—they remind us of all those awful book reports we had to write in third grade. Or maybe because we've been raised not to blow our own horns. This is a mistake. As a business owner, you want to blow your own horn (or whatever the female equivalent expression is) every chance you get. Public relations means getting the attention and love of three audiences: the media, your customers, and the community. All three need to know you are out there and be glad that you are.

Media attention is important because it gives you credibility (whether you deserve it or not). Every time you are in the newspaper, on the radio, or on television, more customers know you exist. More people in the community know you are out there. How do you get the media's attention? The tried and true way is to write the dreaded press release. Once you get the hang of them, they actually can be quite painless. The main thing to remember is that you need to cover:

- What is going on.
- Why it is interesting or unique.
- Who is involved and what that person's role is.
- When the event is taking place (if you are writing about an event).
- Who can be contacted for more information.

I always try to include a photograph and a sample of a product or some other "gift" to get the initial attention of a reporter. P.S.: Don't forget to put a date at the top of the press release so the media will know when it should go into the paper.

The second way to get media coverage is to become a media "pet." The way to do that is to feed reporters information that will make their jobs easier. Like what? Like timely articles about your industry from journals or newspapers they may not see. Or you can provide them with local quotes (from your customers, of course) that reflect a national news story that might be covered over a several-day period. You can give them your own customer-survey responses if you've discovered something you think is interesting. Or you can simply call two or three times a year to suggest a specific news story. Added up, these activities help reporters remember who you are and what you are all about. As a result, yours will be the name they think of when they need a quote to add lines to a story regarding your industry. Better exposure is impossible to get.

Becoming publicly known has all sorts of spin-offs. You may be asked to make speeches in front of audiences of potential customers. I now get more than forty invitations a year. Boards of directors for community groups will want you as a member. You will be asked to be a judge for community events or various contests. All these provide much needed exposure and save you enormous amounts of marketing costs.

Once you have kicked a public relations campaign into gear, you can decide where your money can best be spent getting the attention of your customers. Remember that a customer isn't a customer until she knows you are out there. Now is when you decide to advertise, because your customers will have told you what they read, listen to, and watch. The cardinal rule of advertising is that wherever you decide to advertise, you need to repeat the ad an average of six times before anyone will see it. Ads sort of creep into our consciousness around the fourth time and become imprinted in our brain cells (assuming the advertisement is for a product we are interested in) around time six or seven.

The community is the third side of the triangle. You need to be publicly involved in community organizations. Most women are. The difference now is that your associations need to be consistent with your marketing strategy of exposing yourself to as many customers as you can for the least amount of money and time possible. You'll need to give up being a Girl Scout leader for the treasurer position of the Chamber of Commerce. Or give up teaching church school for involvement in your industry association. To my mind, most women business owners belong to too many organizations. As a result, they miss a lot of meetings and really can't do justice to any one group, which leads to a lousy reputation in the business community. Choose two groups. No more. Focus on them until you've become bored or met all the people you can possibly meet— then you can move onto a different organization.

Summarizing all your marketing ideas is best done in the form of a marketing plan. I offer you the following outline. Add to it as you see fit.

I. Marketing objective

What do you want to accomplish in marketing?

II. Situational analysis

This is where you summarize all the trends discussed earlier in this chapter, as well as the impact they will have on your company.

III. A description of the market

In this section, you outline the size, growth, age and other attributes of the entire market you are after.

IV. The customer

Profile your typical customer in as much detail as you can get. If you can come up with lists of potential customers, put them in here.

V. The competition

Who is your competition? What are their strengths? Their weaknesses?

VI. Market position

What is your uniqueness? Why are you special?

VII. Marketing activities

What marketing activities will you use to get your customers' attention? Here is where you describe your advertising and public relations campaign, how you plan to sell (more on this in the next chapter), and anything else you plan to do that will help bring in revenues. Everyone reading this book should seriously consider attending all pertinent trade shows—as an exhibitor, it's to be hoped, but at a minimum as a participant.

VIII. A timeline

Force yourself to wrap deadlines around all your marketing activities—or they won't get done. This is a fact of life for every entrepreneur. We hate, I repeat *hate*, spending money, and marketing costs money.

SELLING

SUCCESS

Man stand for long time with mouth open before roast duck fly in.
Ancient Chinese Proverb

Any woman who has successfully mated is good at sales. Actually, any woman who has mated is good at selling. For those of you who haven't had happy endings yet, you just need more practice in deciding who your real customer is.

Selling starts with believing in your product—in its quality and timeliness; in what it does. If you aren't convinced that your product is everything it can be, you will never be able to sell it. This is a woman thing. We are terrible liars. In fact, I believe that most women are incapable of lying in business—that has been my experience. So, your first step in selling is to make peace with your product.

What if you aren't sure about it? Over and over I see women hesitating to sell their wares or spending too long in the final stages of product design (for some clients this is becoming a lifetime task). This is a mistake. The trick to developing a saleable product is to "take your best shot" within a specific time frame (that you force yourself to keep—or if you have to, have someone else force you to keep. Bankers are good at this.) and just start selling it.

BELIEVING IN YOUR PRODUCT

More and more women are asking me how to tell if a product is "ready." For women who don't yet trust their intuition on this, I use Faith Popcorn's screen. I love Faith Popcorn. I think she is beyond brilliant, if controversial. Faith's think tanks are made up of constant readers of all the major magazines, kids, and people like you and me who tell her what consumers will want in the near future. And Faith summarizes what she hears for everyone else. And she's right. Usually dead right. Faith's team was the first group to define "cocooning," our penchant for staying home more and entertaining ourselves and our friends at our own hearths. Even though I didn't see cocooning coming, or define it, I have noticed—looking back—that several years ago my friends and I all went from bar hopping and jogging in groups to VCR parties and our own step machines. And, at forty, I even discovered stamp collecting, the perfect cocooning activity for the Nineties.

She's good. And, happily, she has identified what I would call the ten patterns of behavior or thinking that will define what all our customers will want (whether they know it or not) over the next decade: psychographics, fantasy adventure, small indulgences, egonomics, cashing-out, down-aging, staying alive, vigilante consumer, 99 lives, S.O.S. (save our society).

Here's the brilliance of the patterns and the way to build your confidence in your product. If your product is consistent with all the trends identified, then it has a 100 percent probability of saleability. In other words, people will buy it, assuming you can get their attention. If your product is consistent with 90 percent of the trends, there is a 90 percent chance that people will buy it; if it is consistent with 80 percent, the chance is 80 percent, and so on. If you have a product that matches seven or more of these trends, it's time to believe in what you're selling. If it's 50 percent to 60 percent, you need some changes. If it is under 50 percent, you should probably rethink the product completely.

SETTING PRICES

Women price products too low. I remember when I first decided that I wanted to be a consultant, back in the 1980s, I wrote a business plan which pegged my hourly consulting rate at $40 per hour. When my attorney saw that price, he told me to increase it to $60 immediately. There were two reasons. The first was that I would not be able to pay all my bills unless I charged that much. Second, people would not take me seriously at $40 an hour. He was right. And wise. It's a painful, scary lesson, because most of us want to keep our prices low so anyone can afford us. That way we shouldn't have to deal with rejection. But, we're wrong. Most consumers don't look at price first (even though they say they do)—they look at the *quality* of the product and its dependability.

Here's a second story to drive my point home. Years ago, a man I knew who was running for city commissioner stopped me in the street and asked me if I was interested in running his campaign. Since it was something I had never tried, I responded affirmatively. To which he replied, "Fine. Come to my office Monday morning and tell me your price then." Well, I had no idea what the price of a campaign manager was, but I knew what I needed to live on, which was about $600 a month. (See? It really was a long time ago.) That night, on my way to the movies with a friend of mine, I mentioned my job offer and the price I was going to charge. His response was utter disbelief. He bet me that I could charge twice as much and still get the job. The following Monday, I walked into the soon-to-be commissioner's office and asked for $1,200 a month. Without blinking, he said fine and immediately gave me a list of tasks to be done! Looking back, I think I could probably have added another $500 to $600 to my number and still have had the job.

The moral of this story is that whatever price you first set for your product, as a woman you've probably set it too low. When in doubt, charge what your competitors charge (as long as you know you can pay your bills) until you figure out what your customers are truly willing to pay.

Which brings me to the actual act of selling. Of all the skills an entrepreneur needs, this is the first. Selling has a bad name it doesn't deserve. I think that the reason women dislike selling as much as we do is because we have never been quite sure what our customers expect in addition to the actual product purchased (any woman who has had a client ask her to a romantic dinner to "work out the details" knows what I mean). Plus, let's face it, car salesmen have given sales a bad name. But, sales is not forced feeding. Selling is simply a certain type of communication. Selling success comes from being good at finding out what *problems* your potential customer has that you can solve with your product. And getting that discussion going is what makes you money.

Smart service professionals have taught us that there is an *actual structure* to the sales process. In its most simple form, selling can be divided into two phases. The first phase consists of finding out everything you can about your prospective customer so you understand his or her (or their) needs. Phase two is presenting yourself as the solution they are looking for.

It turns out that the more you plan, the more successful you will be. Although I learned much of how to sell from IBM training in the late 1960s, more recently I was reminded of the truths of selling success from an extraordinary woman, Jan Farnsworth, who spends her days teaching accountants how to sell. Believe me, if accountants can learn to sell successfully, anyone can.

Jan defines the sales process as having six steps:

1. Planning
2. Understanding the needs of your customer
3. Planning again
4. Designing a solution
5. Obtaining the clients' conviction that you have the solution
6. Getting the customer to act

PLANNING

No matter what you are selling—whether it's a service or a widget—you need to plan. Your first step is to decide what your goal is. For some readers it will be to get a contract to evaluate management quality for someone, and for others of you it will be to bring a new toy to the market. When I'm about to approach a company on any level, I always try to find out if Deloitte & Touche has worked with similar companies on similar projects so I first can get some hints about the real needs of the company. Then, I become an obsessed woman, finding out everything I can about the company. A side point here: I use only ethical methods to discover what I can because, in the end, there probably is a hell and I'm not interested in spending time there just because I pretended I was a graduate student doing market research to get some data somewhere. Besides, I think most people know when you're lying to them.

Back to selling. There are many, many sources of information about your potential customers: newspaper articles, Dun & Bradstreet reports, people you may know who are their employees, their public relations department. Once you've discovered as much as you think you can, you can sit down and make some pretty informed guesses about what is going on in the company (or in the lives of the customers if you are selling to people).

The types of guesses you need to make should include:

- Their service needs (if you are selling a service)
- How they make decisions
- What motivates them
- How you think they'll make the decision to use you
- How satisfied they are with what they are currently using
- When is the best time to approach them

Once you have the lay of this land, trust your intuition. (Have I told you to trust your intuition too often yet? If not, trust it. Here especially. You'll be amazed at how close you'll come to what is actually going on. Sometimes this experience gets to feel a lot like being in the Twilight Zone, but go with it anyway.)

I was raised to be prepared so I always list the questions I plan to ask a potential customer before I ask them. That way, I don't have to worry about forgetting anything. At the same time, I put myself in the other person's shoes so I can anticipate how he or she will respond, especially focusing on objections. The first time you sell your product, if you are like I was, you'll panic when you hear your first objections. It took me years to realize that objections are actually the first phase of buying into a product. As a woman, that can be hard to swallow since we haven't been socialized to put ourselves out there so we can get objections. Instead, we wait until we're dead sure we have something and *then* go after it. At least that's the modus operandi of all us ex-debutantes—we're all clinging to the notion that selling should be smooth, gentle, and without argument or emotion when, in fact, we should be going for the opposite. We *want* our customers to be emotional. We *want* to be able to argue about the benefits we bring to their table. We *want* them to want our product and to be miserably disappointed if they don't have it! In the beginning, you may want to role play a sales call several times just to get the "rhythm" of it. Try to pick friends or associates whose response to your words will come close to your real customer.

Gather references about you as well. They build courage. The best salespeople I know actually have a photo album filled with letters of appreciation and other kudos. They can then simply turn to the appropriate "Thank God you were here" letter when they need it. If you don't have letters, you can make a mental list of former customers who would give you high marks and, when it is time, don't be afraid to name names. In the 1990s, personal references will become increasingly important as sales tools. With so much information coming at each of us, we will depend more and more on the opinions of people we know.

To be on the safe side (and because they taught me this in graduate school), I also think hard about who else will be trying to sell a solution to my potential customers, anticipating their sales points so I'll be able to talk about them when I meet with the customer.

There are hundreds of books on sales. It's worth your time to head for your favorite bookstore and pick out a few to buy and read. Zig Ziglar is a great motivational sales coach; so is Brian Tracey. There are many more—most are worth at least a quick read.

The best introduction to a potential client is through someone who knows both of you. I have tried all kinds of selling, from cold calling on the telephone to dropping in unexpectedly to using an associate's name as a referral. As a woman who has a low tolerance for rejection, I have to say that cold calling is terrible. I know that there are people out there (my luck one of you is reading this now) who thrive on cold calling. For most women, it's just too much rejection. So, get introductions. In other words, you want to target companies or distributors (if you are selling through someone else to your end customer) where you know somebody who can give you an introduction. In twelve years, *I have never been turned down* when I call someone to meet with them if I have a name of a mutual acquaintance as a referral. Never. Now, this doesn't mean that I've always made the sale, but that was my own learning curve ticking away. You want referrals. In fact, you want referrals from everyone who knows the caliber of your work. Don't hesitate to ask. Satisfied customers expect it. Business associates expect it. Your service professionals expect it. And, if you are good at what you do (and you are or you wouldn't be spending time reading this book to get better!), they'll be glad to make the referral—*for your customers' sake*. So ask. Many women treat this task with as much fear and trepidation as asking for a date. Maybe we're afraid of rejection. Maybe we don't realize how good we are. Just remember, it's not the same thing. So ask. Ask everybody. And then thank them as you get the business.

THE SALES MEETING

Most sales coaches list a number of goals for sales meetings. I have only three. You need to:

1. Establish rapport.
2. Find out what the other person's needs are related to your product.
3. Sell your solution (or at least a step toward your solution). An example of this might be a second meeting where you make a formal proposal to serve the client.

You already know what rapport is. It's getting onto someone else's wave length—feeling as if you're talking the same language. Women are good at this—with one caveat. We may do too much of this. I hope my own experience will tell you what I mean.

When I first started "selling" for Deloitte & Touche, I would team up with one of our partners as his mentee. Well. I happen to be very interested in people. What that meant in our meetings is that I would chat happily away with our prospective clients . . . never quite getting to the point. After several lunches, the partner suggested that I control or limit my interest to about ten minutes. My immediate reaction was that this would make us appear to be cold, greedy, and self-interested in the extreme. I was wrong. Instead, I learned to find one or two things we had in common with the prospective client, chat a bit, and get on to business. And I did just fine. So don't overdo it.

Which brings me to the next sales street smarts. The best way to find out what your client's or potential client's needs are is to ask questions. Lots of them. In fact, sales coaches tell me that more than half of the words out of your mouth should be in the form of questions that, it's hoped, will confirm your guesses about the company's needs. Or, if they don't, at least you'll find out what the real needs are.

When you think about it, asking questions makes intuitive sense. Doctors have a great deal of authority. Why? Partly their training is responsible. Partly it is because when a doctor walks into an examining room he or she spends a great deal of time asking questions. And our reaction as patients? Right or wrong, we see them as the experts. Questions have that impact. So ask questions. Lots.

As any communications expert knows (and the rest of us don't), there are basically two types of questions: open-ended and closed-ended. Open-ended questions tend to be broad and usually require long answers. My favorite is "How's business?" and "What brought you to the decision to talk with us?" Others I often use are:

- What are your future plans for the company?
- How has your business changed in the past year?
- Who will decide whether to use our product?
- What do you need the product to do?

- How long do you need to make a decision about _____?
- When did you discover you had a problem with _____?

Most questions that start out with "what," "why," or "how" are open-ended questions. On average, I try to ask at least eight to ten of these (instead of telling people my life story, which is what I really want to do), focusing on the people or the person in the company who is the customer, what specific needs he has that I'm trying to meet, and how decisions are made.

Closed-ended questions can easily be answered with one word, "yes" or "no." If you watch a good salesperson, you will notice that she uses this type of questions to paraphrase what she's heard (to make sure she's heard it right) and to confirm something about the prospective client:

- So the president of the company makes all the decisions about supplies?
- So you only buy from catalogs if you can use a charge card?
- Did I hear you correctly, red Ferraris are the only cars that interest you?
- Are you saying that if Volkswagen brought back the Beetle you would buy one?

There are many, many benefits to asking questions. They:

- Confirm what you thought.
- Tell you the person's priorities.
- Tell you if you are dealing with a time line.
- Tell you what the client's expectations are.
- Help you to figure out what is motivating the person. Is it survival? Security? Power? Adventure? Achievement?
- Build your own confidence in your solution.
- Help you to figure out how to position your product as the solution to their problem.

- Show that you are interested.
- Demonstrate the pertinent opinions of the prospective client.
- Give you a chance to demonstrate your expertise.
- Help to develop rapport—the better questions you ask the more your client or customer will trust you.

When should you stop asking questions? When you know the answers to the following questions:

- What does the person need?
- Does she know she needs it?
- How will she decide what will fulfill the need?
- If she isn't the decision maker, who is? (Brace yourself here. If she isn't the decision maker, you need to do this whole dance again—with the real decision maker.)

Which brings me to a corollary truth about selling. Always have at least two good suits, because you never know when you'll need to repeat your sales call. The woman who started *Parents* magazine has a wonderful story about this. As I remember it, she had made a presentation to Time, Inc. to invest in her magazine. Although her presentation was very good, she had spent more than a year bootstrapping the magazine start-up out of her own funds and was down to one decent suit. You can imagine her chagrin when she was asked to repeat her performance! So, do what you have to, but make sure you have more than one suit.

Back to the questions you should have answered:

- Who will pay for your product?
- Is this an important decision to the customer and why?
- Who is competing with you?

How long should all this take? No more than an hour at the most. Remember, time is the currency of the 1990s—I can usually get my questions answered in a half hour or so. *Keep the meeting short and sweet.* This is especially important for women, because people don't expect us to do that. I'm on several boards of directors, which means that every year I'm being the president for some organization somewhere. I start on time and I finish on time—to the minute. Inevitably, someone thanks me and expresses surprise. The trick is to know what questions you want to get answered *before* you go into any meeting. And I've found that people are happy to see you come in with a list as long as you tell them it is to ask them source questions you have prepared to save them time.

As an entrepreneur, you will have numerous to-do lists running through your head all the time. As a woman, you'll have extra ones related to children (if you have them), mates (if you have them), and household chores. In selling, it's important to put these on hold so you can LISTEN to your customer's answers. The worst thing you can do is to get distracted so you don't hear an answer. Why? Because if you have to ask for the answer again, it will look as if you don't care what is being said (think about your own life—doesn't it make you crazy when you are talking to someone and suddenly realize that they aren't hearing a word you are saying!).

Worse, if you don't ask the person to repeat what he or she just said, you could miss critical information that could make or break your sale.

Watch for the blocks. They come in all shapes and sizes.

Distractions are one. Personal distractions range from mentally writing notes to your child's schoolteacher to sexual fantasies. The latter are the absolute worst distractions because even when you realize you aren't paying attention you don't want to stop. People who speak with different accents, speed, and style are very difficult to listen to. To-do lists are constant saboteurs. Thinking ahead also gets in your way, especially when you find yourself designing your solution to the person's problem before you've heard the story. Faking it is deadly too. I hesitate here to get into a long discussion about how we women are good at faking it, because I don't want anyone using it against me in my old age. Let me just say this. Any woman who has ever had a small child chattering away at her has become an expert at "fake listening." You know who you are. The problem arises when we are sitting there nodding and smiling only to have the potential customer say "What do you think?" If you don't have a relevant answer, you've just lost the sale.

Ego also gets in our way. While the thought "this guy is so stupid" may be a fairly accurate description of the person to whom you are selling, it does not make a sale. Be careful. If your ego gets in your way, you will come across as arrogant and, dare I say, bitchy—when neither, of course, is true. You probably are smarter than the other person, but if you show it, the sale won't happen.

The only way I know to listen well is to take notes. Not just any notes, but a list of key words that will help me to really analyze what's going on and to look for what will lead to a "yes." There are a wide variety of formats these notes could take. Here's the one I use:

Name of Company _____ Date _____

Key Concern?	What Solution Do We Have?	What Benefits to Customer?
1.		
2.		
3.		
4.		
5.		
6.		
7.		
8.		

While I'm writing, I'm also thinking about what proof I have available to back up any points I want to make. It could be letters of reference from happy customers, or testimonials, charts, graphs, surveys, and so forth.

Even though on some days I think we've become a nation of whiners, when you really listen you'll discover that most potential customers have only a handful of key concerns. When you get to a point in your conversation where it feels as if you have enough information, stop. If you aren't sure when that is, you can wait until the person starts repeating himself or herself. Then you can stop. Take the time to summarize what you've heard to make sure you really have been in the room. This is very affirming to the potential client. It shows how important his words have been to you.

At this point, you have two choices. You can either ask for the business or ask to come back if you need additional information from someone else. If you do need to talk to other people, the exercise is the same.

What if you have enough information? What if you know what the potential customer's needs are? What if you know that you have the solutions to his problems? What if you've figured out what will get the "yes"?

ASK FOR THE SALE. We hate to do this. I can remember a sales training class where the instructor told us that her firm had videotaped sales calls, and in more than 85 percent of the cases the salesperson never asked for the sale! This was true for men and women.

Why? Because we hate rejection. All of us. And when you ask for a sale, there is always the chance that the person sitting across from you will say no. Virtually every business owner I know can tell a story of her first sales experiences and the tears it took to get past the no's. One of my associates used to focus sales calls on skyscraper-type buildings so she could go sit in the stairwells between floors and cry between calls. She used to end her day when her eyes were too swollen and puffy to hide with makeup. Now she is a sales addict—she lives to sell—and loves it, because she discovered a sales truth that every good salesperson knows: *it's never personal.* A no never has anything to do with you personally. Ever. Once that realization sinks in, selling becomes more of a mystery tour where you get to see who will say yes and who will say no. The more experience you get, the faster those yes responses will pick up.

There are lots of sales trainers out there to coach you. Zig Ziglar came out of IBM in the years when IBM had the best sales training ever. The situations he lived through make anything that you or I will experience child's play. His street smarts are wonderfully enlightening. Two truths I remember from him are these:

Most salespeople hear nine no's before they get to a yes. What that means is that every time you hear a no (assuming you have a good product), you want to thank the person, knowing you are that much closer to a yes. (Plus, in my experience, some of those no's will turn into a yes later as people think more about your product.)

The second truth is this. Eighty percent of your sales will come from 20 percent of your clients. If you pay attention, you will soon identify those 20 percent. They should get most of your attention. And, you should go for repeats. Once someone buys, unless you totally mess up they will buy again and again.

Once you have the sale, you're almost home. Here's what solidifies the relationship: saying thank you. Women are good at this. Here's what I mean. Elaine Moncur was one of my role models. For years she was a teacher. Then she became a distributor for Apple. When I met her, she was the most successful businesswoman I had ever met. When I asked her why, she said she thanked her customers, and not just verbally. Whenever she got a signed contract from someone, the next day she would send that person (male or female) a bouquet of flowers thanking the person for the business and expressing her excitement at working with him or her. The result: unbelievable success. She had started off the relationship on a strong positive note and kept it there with ongoing personal notes and small gifts that kept her way out in front of all her competitors. Once I hired her firm to do an all-day marketing seminar for about twenty-five of my clients. We held it in a community college where the food was, let's say edible, but that's about it. Elaine showed up with bouquets of fresh flowers to brighten up the room and a van full of fresh fruit so everyone could happily munch their way through the day with oranges, bananas, apples, kiwis, and even some fruit I don't recognize to this day. You won't be surprised when I tell you that she received the highest marks any seminar has ever received—straight tens out of ten. That is what selling success is. Listening, proposing a solution to the customer's problems, thanking them, and overproducing. Women are very good at all of these—once we get past our fear of rejection. So get past it. Let your mantra be "there's no such thing as rejection" (since there isn't) and you will be a raging success at sales. Honest.

YOU WON'T

ALWAYS BE

30–SOMETHING

TOOLS FOR RETIREMENT

But for three outstanding women, I would have never made it through this chapter. Diane Farber, vice president of Prudential Securities in Ann Arbor, taught me everything I now know about financial planning. Barbara Spalding from Spalding Associates in Princeton kept me in newsletters that guided me through tax specifics, and Joan Fisher Glenn in Voorhees, New Jersey, I'm sure spent half of her FAX allowance keeping me in estate-planning guidelines.

You'll get tired. You'll grow old. Somewhere around year five of business ownership you'll start to fantasize about a way out—even if you really *love* what you are doing. To prepare for that day—because it really does seem to hit women suddenly— you need to do three things for yourself. The first is to understand your own personal finances—when money comes in and when it goes out; when it's yours and when it's the government's; where it is; and how much you have. The second is to have accumulated a stash of cash, because what you may be experiencing might be real burnout and not your first pangs of lusting for retirement. You won't know until you've taken off two weeks (by yourself) so you can sit still and figure out what is really going on. The third thing is a real retirement plan—a step-by-step path to freedom from your business when you are ready.

UNDERSTANDING YOUR FINANCES

The first rule of retirement is to keep your personal finances *separate* from business. If you've had good accounting advice, you'll know that most of the expenses in your life as an entrepreneur really are business expenses and you've categorized them accordingly. Even so, you need a *personal* monthly budget that shows you when money comes in and how you are using it. What does this imply? That you need to *give yourself an income*. It can be small. It can be deferred. It can be in the form of government bonds for your yet-to-be-conceived grandchild. Just do it. There are actually some psychological reasons for this. An income shows progress. It's a reward, however small, for your hard work. It connotes freedom of choice. It's a burnout preventative.

If you can control your amount of personal income and want it to stay small so you can grow the business, that's fine. It keeps you right up there with all the great entrepreneurs in history. Just make sure you pay yourself enough to pay your bills *and save for retirement*.

If you aren't really sure what you need (which is true for all of us at first), now is the time to figure out your personal monthly budget, preferably on a computer, using a spreadsheet similar to the one you have in your office. On the spreadsheet, you need to start with your monthly income, summarizing:

AMOUNT
SOURCE
HOW LONG WILL IT CONTINUE

The continuation factor is very important. Say you have child support payments, or you're living off Aunt Lucy's will, or you have royalties from a book you wrote for other women in your industry. They will come to an end. You'll need to see for yourself when you think that will happen so you don't slide from almost middle class to poor again as a result of losing that check.

Once you figure out your income, analyze how you spend it. I do this in two steps: first the "musts" that I believe I simply cannot live without (and I suggest you follow my categories) and then the "because I want to" category. If your "because I want to" expenses are as much as the musts, worry not. It's a female thing. I say that as long as you have an income that covers everything, go ahead and do what you want to do. You just need to know where you'll be able to cut when you decide enough is enough or if the business goes through a stumbling period.

MUST-PAY EXPENSES

Housing	(This is your main residence, not the cabin in Vermont, not the condo in New Mexico.)
	—Mortgage
	—Utilities
	—Replacement of old/broken stuff
Food	(This is everything but business-related meals.)
	—Food
	—Vitamins
	—Filtered water
Clothes	—Business
	—Play
	—Exercise
	—Makeup
	—Hair costs

Car	(This is normally a business expense and probably should be for you. Talk to your accountant and don't lose the opportunity to buy those magnetic signs you can slap onto the side of your car by day and take off at night and on the weekends when it's okay for people not to recognize you.) —Gas —Maintenance
Health Insurance	(Again, the business should pay for this.)
Massage	(Just write it down, okay? If you haven't ever had a massage, go try one—barter for it if you don't have the money—it's one of the most immediate stress relievers known to humans, which helps you to stay healthy. I'm told that massages also help to prevent you from frying out your immune system.)
Parenting Costs	—Clothes for children —Day-care/baby-sitter for a date once a week —Health costs —Toys
Retirement	(This is a must—start small if you have to. You'll need this sooner than you know. Just think of how fast this last year went for you. Well, the next years will be even faster!)
Vacation	(Ditto. You need a vacation every year. If you can manage to save only $80, go to a local hotel on their annual Valentine's Day sale and sit in a jacuzzi until your skin is totally wrinkled and you almost fall asleep.)
Because I Want to	—Presents —Things you really don't need generally —Books/magazines —Charitable donations

Then add 10 percent of your monthly total, because there will be something that neither of us has thought about. When you figure out your budget, also try to guess how much it will grow or contract over time. For example, your child-care costs should decrease over time. On the other hand, health and food costs may go up if you become a healthier food eater.

The main point here is that you really need to understand how your personal dollars cycle their way through your life before you can properly plan for retirement.

DANCING WITH THE INTERNAL REVENUE SERVICE

They terrify us. We never ever want to have to sit face-to-face with an IRS agent—ever. So what do we do? We hesitate out of fear to write off expenses that are legitimate business expenses. Stop. It's okay to dance with the IRS. You have a good accountant. Let her worry about dealing with them. In the meantime, you need to start tracking money you are spending for the business so you can legitimately decrease your taxes, because the expenses are deducted from your income. (It's not dollar for dollar, but anything helps.) The result will feel a little like a raise. Until your subconscious realizes that you now have more money to spend on you, stash your "savings" in a retirement account.

So what is a legitimate business expense? Although this changes every year, there are some general guidelines you can follow *under the guidance of your accountant*. The point is that once you know them, you need to track them.

Let's start with your home office. Use that room or space *only* as an office and you have a legitimate business expense.

Now your car. It's a business expense unless you use someone else's car to do your business chores, and I don't know anyone who does that. You can basically deduct all "operating and fixed" costs related to using your car. This includes depreciation (that is, the amount less your car is worth at the end of the year), maintenance, repairs, tires, gas, oil, insurance, license plates, parking fees, and tolls! In other words, a lot. A trip to the spa's worth. The trick is to track expenses. This is a pain, but a worthwhile one. At worst, you can make photocopies of the following chart below and keep it in your car.

CAR MILEAGE AND OPERATING EXPENSES

Date	Destination-Purpose of Trip—Contact	Odometer Begin End	Business	Investment	Personal	Gas, Oil, Lube	Parking—Tolls	Other	Describe

You can also get deductions for your computer. If your computer is used exclusively at your office, then you can write off expenses related to it, like depreciation. If, on the other hand, you share your computer with other members of your family, you can still get some write-off. Just keep a log of how you use the computer and figure out how much of that time was spent for personal things, like writing your annual Christmas letter. A chart like this will help:

COMPUTER TIME LOG

Date	Purpose	Business Use Time in Hours	Personal Use Time in Hours
	TOTAL TIME		
	PERCENTAGE PERSONAL USE		%

You can also deduct a portion of business entertainment and gifts. Here you need to keep a verifiable record (in other words, keep your receipts!) of the (1) amount of the expense, (2) the time and place of the travel or entertainment, (3) the date and description of the gift, and (4) the purpose as it relates to your business and the business relationship of the person you entertained or who received the present. Even hotel expenses can be included as long as you document, document, document. My colleagues at Deloitte & Touche tell me that you really need to keep only "documentary evidence" of expenses of $25 or more, but I'm more compulsive than that. I keep everything. It's all listed out on my VISA bills anyway, so I might as well keep them.

If you don't already have an expense-recordkeeping system as a part of your Franklin planner or Day Timer, the following chart should help.

Date	Function or Gift	Place	Purpose	Business Relationship	Cost
	TOTAL:				

At the end of the year, you can take all your information and summarize it for your accountant. The following charts were taken out of Deloitte & Touche's Business Expense Log:

RECAP SHEETS
19__ Recap of Car Mileage & Expenses

Month	Mileage Breakdown			Expenses		
	Business	Investment	Personal	Gas, Oil, Lube	Parking—Tolls	Other
January						
February						
March						
April						
May						
June						
July						
August						
September						
October						
November						
December						
Totals						

Total Car Expenses: $_____

1993 Recap of Other Business Expenses

Month	Entertainment	Meals	Lodging	Fares	Other
January					
February					
March					
April					
May					
June					
July					
August					
September					
October					
November					
December					
Subtotal					
Limitation*	80%	80%			
Totals					

Total Other Business Expenses $_____

---

*Deductions for entertainment and business meals are limited to 80 percent of the expenses—however, this limitation does not apply to (1) reimbursed expenses of employees and (2) expenses that are deductible as compensation. If the 80 percent limit applies to your entertainment and meal expenses, multiply the amounts shown on the "Subtotal" lines by the 80 percent "Limitation" in order to arrive at your deductible expenses.

REIMBURSEMENT RECORD
19__ Record of Reimbursements

Month	Car Operating Expenses	Other Business Expenses
January		
February		
March		
April		
May		
June		
July		
August		
September		
October		
November		
December		
Totals		

Total 19__ Reimbursements $_____

19__ BUSINESS EXPENSE RECAP

Total Car Expenses $_____
Total Other Business Expenses $_____
Total 19__ Business Expenses $_____
Less Reimbursements $_____
Net 19__ Business Expenses $_____

Postscript. Everything that has to do with the government changes *all the time* including allowable expenses. Keep posted by using your attorney and accountant.

WHY YOU NEED STASHES OF CASH

Because emergencies come up. Because situations change. Because you need a break. Because your kid needs braces and the dentist wants a cash advance.

How much? Well, in the olden days (before charge cards), our parents told us that we should have six months of living expenses in the bank at any one time. Just in case. These days, with interest rates the way they are, keeping that kind of money in the bank is equivalent to losing money. You make only a tiny bit of interest, if you make any at all, on money that could be put to better use. So. My advice is a new millennium version on an old theme. You still need to figure out the amount of six months of "have to have" expenses. Then go and get a *personal line of credit* from your bank for that amount. Let your stashes of cash be someone else's until you need it. I'll use me as an example. Part of the pleasure of living in a small town in the Midwest is that I could make it through six months on about $10,000. It wouldn't be fun, but I could do it. So, I went to my credit union and gradually built up a line of credit for $10,000. It's there when I need it and I don't have to pay interest on it unless I actually use it. You can and should do the same thing. VISA cards also work, but the interest rates are so high that just about any other source of cash is cheaper. So find a stash you can tap now—before you need it.

RETIREMENT PLANNING

The statistics tell a grim story. According to the U.S. Department of Commerce, only 50 percent of all Americans are financially independent at age sixty-five. Seventy-five percent end up depending on family, friends, bartering, and social security to make ends meet. More than 25 percent have to work beyond retirement just to make ends meet. It's not a happy picture. For you to be comfortable later, you will probably need $30,000 a year or more to live on—and more if you plan to have any fun at all. What does this mean? That you need to resolve to start planning and saving for retirement today. Not tomorrow. Or Friday, or next year. I'm sure you've already seen the articles in all the women's magazines that show how saving a couple hundred dollars a month at age thirty is equivalent to saving a thousand or more at age forty or more. The moral of the story— the sooner you start saving the better.

What will social security cover? Nothing, unless you work a required number of years and earn a certain amount of credits. According to Joan Fisher Glenn, the credit is called "quarter of coverage," and you earn a maximum of four per year, one for each $570 you earn. Most people need about forty credits before they can receive any monthly benefits at all when they retire. As I write, the average monthly social security benefit for a retired worker is $629.50, and the maximum monthly benefit someone retiring this year at age sixty-five would get is $1,088. As you can see, you'll need to supplement any social security you do get.

There are as many ways to plan for retirement as there are financial planners. Find yourself an adviser, someone you trust, to tell your vision, goals, and fears to. Find someone who will figure out a way to force you to save, because you won't be able to force yourself. There are just too many things that need your attention and cash for you to be able to peel your fingers off your income without help.

The following questionnaire, provided to me by Diane Farber at Prudential Securities, will help you to get started in your thinking.

RETIREMENT PLANNING QUESTIONNAIRE

	Yourself	Spouse
1. What is your date of birth?	/ /	/ /
2. At what age do you expect to retire?	_____	_____
3. What is the current value of your retirement plans?	$_____	$_____
4. What annual pretax benefits do you expect to receive from your company pension plan(s)? (N/A if you are not covered by an employer pension plan.)	$_____	$_____
5. Are these benefit(s) indexed to inflation? (Y/N)	_____	_____
6. What are your annual contributions to retirement plans (401(k) plans, etc.)? (Include both your savings and savings made on your behalf by employers.)	$_____	$_____
7. What is your current annual income?	$_____	$_____
8. What is the total value of other assets available for retirement? Liquid Assets:	$_____	$_____
Investment Assets:	$_____	$_____
9. What are your estimated current living expenses?	$_____	
10. What is your annual retirement spending goal in today's dollars?	$_____	
11. What overall pretax rate of return do you expect to earn on your investments?	_____%	

Now you know the need. Where can you start to stash? Until you know better, start putting everything you can into an individual retirement account (IRA). You can contribute $2,000 a year to an IRA, as of this writing.

IRA Deduction Chart for Taxes

Filing Status	Modified Adjusted Gross Income	Allowable IRA Deduction
Single	$25,000 or less	Full deduction
	Over $25,000 but less than $35,000	Partial Deduction
	$35,000 or more	No deduction
Married Filing Jointly	$40,000 or less	Full deduction
	Over $40,000 but less than $50,000	Partial Deduction
	$50,000 or more	No deduction
Married Filing Separately*	Over-0-but less than $10,000	Partial Deduction
	$10,000 or more	No deduction

*If married filing separately and you were not covered by a plan but your spouse was, you are considered covered by a plan if you lived with your spouse at any time during the year.

Source: Prudential Securities Retirement and Financial Consulting Division

Find an institution that will let you pay into it if you can and then take *that money off the top of your income*—even if it is only $50 a month. That's how I started. Even if you don't qualify for tax deductions on IRAs, they are still effective, because they give you the benefit of tax-deferred growth, which means that your IRAs will grow faster than if you stashed your money in a savings account (because savings accounts are taxable).

The following chart shows you what I mean:

THE BENEFITS OF TAX-DEFERRED INVESTING

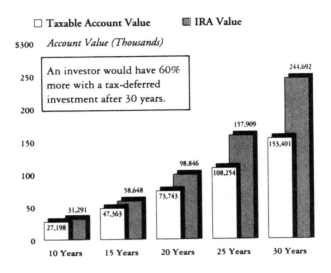

□ Taxable Account Value   ■ IRA Value

$300   *Account Value (Thousands)*

An investor would have 60% more with a tax-deferred investment after 30 years.

	10 Years	15 Years	20 Years	25 Years	30 Years
Taxable Account Value	27,198	47,363	73,743	108,254	153,401
IRA Value	31,291	58,648	98,846	157,909	244,692

Assumes an 8 percent Annual Rate of Return and $2,000 Annual Contribution. Taxable account is based on a 31 percent tax bracket.

Source: Prudential Securities Financial Planning Department

As a business owner, you can also set up a 401(k) program or Simplified Employee Pension Plan (SEP), which allows you and your employees to make tax-deductible retirement contributions into a pot that continues to grow until you retire or choose to leave the company. These days you can contribute up to 15 percent of each employee's compensation or $30,000 per year in an SEP. There's even something called a Salary Reduction SEP (SARSEP), which is like a mini-401(k) program for companies with twenty-five or fewer employees. Almost $9,000 can be invested in the SARSEP (or a 401(k) program for that matter) on a pretax basis *by each employee,* or by them and you, *every year.*

That's how to save for retirement! The "pot" then invests that money for all of you.

And don't be afraid to buy stocks and bonds. Coca-Cola isn't going anywhere. Neither is Ford. You *want* to buy stocks and bonds as a retirement investment program. Which ones depends on the amount of risk you can tolerate without lying awake at night wondering how your money is doing. A good financial planner will teach you how to invest in a broad range of stocks and/or bonds that will protect you, short of any national or international crisis that none of us will survive. She'll also help you to match your investments with your financial needs. People usually buy stocks in companies as a longer-term strategy, and then invest in bonds and money markets when they need to use their money sooner. The following list gives you an idea of the range that is out there!

- *Government securities* offer the highest degree of safety available and provide predictable income.

- *Municipal bonds* are good for investors looking for current income exempt from federal taxes.

- *Corporate bonds* afford a degree of safety while providing a high level of income.

- *Mutual funds* are an easy way to invest in well-diversified, professionally managed portfolios.

- *Stocks* provide the opportunity to share a corporation's assets while receiving dividend income.

- *Annuities* can allow your earnings to accumulate tax-deferred until they're withdrawn.

Source: Prudential Securities, *Don't Let Your Money Retire with You*

The choices are endless. And entertaining. And you can overlay your values to choose the types of investments you want to make. For example, I am very biased toward companies who have women and multiple ethnic groups on their boards of directors, because I know that ethnic "diversity" and managing and coping with that diversity will be an issue of the 1990s for all companies. That a company has diversified its board tells me it will have an advantage over its competitors who don't—and I want to be in on that smart management style.

EXAMPLES OF INVESTMENT OPPORTUNITIES

- Common stocks
- Taxable corporate bonds
- Tax-free municipal bonds
- Zero coupon bonds
- Annuities (variable and fixed rate)
- Unit trusts
- Professionally managed investment programs such as
  —Mutual funds
  —Independent managed money programs

The point is to get some money working for you now. No, I'm not done. The last lap is your

ESTATE PLANNING

As a business owner, you face two truths. You will die and you will pay taxes. We face taxes much better than we face death—but that doesn't make them go away. If you want to make sure that your company will survive you and that your family will be taken care of, you need an estate plan. There are five parts to any effective estate plan:

1. A plan for transferring your assets to your family members in a way that is both orderly and creates the least amount of tax liabilities possible.

2. A designation of who will take over the company when you are gone, and this should include compensation plans geared to continue hiring the best people the company can afford.

3. Sufficient insurance to keep your company going.

4. Up-to-date financial arrangements so sources of capital for the firm will be obvious.

5. A valuation of the company in case it has to be sold.

The most critical component of an effective estate plan is a properly prepared will—one that transfers your assets in accordance with your wishes. Additionally, you need to consider the probate process and the possible tax liabilities of your estate. Your accountant can help you go through all the issues related to your estate.

Once you've developed a plan designed to accomplish your goals, you should review the plan annually to ensure that it is still effective. Personal changes, such as increased net worth, marriage, divorce, or the birth of a child, could make your present plan unworkable. Estate and income-tax-law changes could also make your present plan less effective.

YOUR WILL

Writing a will protects your family and ensures that your wishes will be carried out. Anyone of legal age with any property at all should have a will. If you die without a will, or what is known as intestate, your estate will be distributed as determined by state law and administered by someone appointed by the court. Dying intestate can also increase the tax burden for your heirs and cause all sorts of problems for your family.

A will lets you:

- Distribute your property as you wish, including personal property of sentimental value.
- Provide for future management of investments for your business.
- Designate guardians for your minor children.
- Select the person you want to distribute your estate, eliminating the necessity of an expensive, court-appointed administrator.
- Minimize taxes and administration expenses in the settlement of your estate.
- Provide for special needs, such as charitable contributions.

LIFE INSURANCE

Life insurance is an essential estate planning tool because it provides immediate cash for survivors. Since proceeds are readily available, life insurance protects your family from being forced to liquidate some of your other assets to meet living expenses. Life insurance can also help your survivors pay debts, including estate taxes. Generally, insurance passes directly to the beneficiary and does not have to go through the probate process.

ESTATE TAX RULES

Here are some estate tax rules from Joan Fisher Glenn. You may need them.

Annual Exclusions: Any person can give up to $10,000 per year to any other person, and such a gift will be totally excluded from any calculation of taxable gifts. There is no limit on the number of people to whom such gifts can be made. Thus, a parent can give $10,000 to each child, to each grandchild, and to any other person he or she wants to, free of any gift tax consequences. Such a gift, if properly made, will also be free of any generation-skipping transfer tax consequences.

A husband and wife together can give $20,000 per year to any individual. If the money all comes from one spouse, the other spouse can join in the gift (by signing the appropriate line on a gift tax return) to take advantage of both spouses' annual exclusions.

Annual exclusion gifts must be "present interests." This means that the gift must be made outright, to a custodial account under the Uniform Gift to Minors Act, or to a trust that has certain provisions specifically qualifying it for the exclusion. Typically, these provisions either allow the beneficiary of the trust to withdraw the gift to the trust for a limited period of time or, in the case of a person under twenty-one, require that all the funds in the trust be payable to the beneficiary when he or she attains the age of twenty-one.

The Marital Deduction: Gifts between spouses are entirely exempt from any transfer tax so long as they are made outright or in a trust that meets certain requirements. Lifetime transfers between spouses can be important for taking advantage of estate and generation-skipping tax exemptions.

You can also shelter income through a marital deduction, charitable deductions, and keeping your taxable estate under $600,000. Get help from your accountant on the fine-line rules related to all this. My only point is that you need to plan.

CHAPTER 12

*D*ON'T

POSTPONE JOY

(or)

TAKING CARE OF YOURSELF

Be careful reading health books. You may die from a misprint.
Mark Twain

FIRST KNOW YOURSELF

Prepare for the worst. You'll get sick. Be angry. Learn to live with frustration. Wonder why you ever thought your mate was the sexiest person in the universe. Stress will be your monster—and it's one you'll need to tame to survive business, physically and emotionally. How? Although there are as many ways to deal with stress as there are therapists and *Cosmo* writers, in the interest of saving your time, here is what I know. You need to first know yourself. Who you are influences the way you feel, cope and manage. It's worth your time, before you get too far along on this business owner trail, to figure out what your real life goals are (on a personal level as well as a professional level), to figure out what you do best (so you can delegate out the rest of your tasks), and where your real values are. This exercise will help you to predict where stress will come from. For example, if your deepest value is honesty and integrity, don't start a business in an industry that is known for its dishonesty. Or if you do, know that you will face constant stress as you confront a value system that isn't your match. You'll be able to plan your massages around the meetings with your supplier or investor or whoever else it is that is causing that tension in your shoulders. So know yourself and where your hot spots will be. One of the results is that you will increase your capacity to take risks (a skill set critical to any burgeoning business), since you'll trust your own judgment more and more.

Four parts of you need to stay healthy—your physical you, your mental you, your emotional you, and your spiritual self. Here's what I mean. If you don't take care of each part, you'll get sick. Not just a little sick . . . a lot sick. Serious sick. I've seen it. The women who balance their personal lives *by not becoming too obsessed* about any one area of their lives—including their business— tend not to experience physical ailments, not to mention those emotional lows that attack the rest of us. *Your top priority must be balance.* Even if, in the end, you have to give up your company.

Here's how. I'll start with the easy stuff first. Pick a church, any church (or temple, or ashram, or sangha . . .). One that won't be judgmental toward you and the fact that you are a business owner. This sounds easier than it is—you may need to try out several different religious traditions before you find one that affirms you and your choice of business ownership. Then practice that religion.

Next, let go of your sick friends. They are the ones who whine, who let you know that you never quite meet their expectations because you're always late or they don't see you enough. The same truth holds for family members. You cannot emotionally afford to have people who are putting you down close to you. It's mental suicide. Decide what you want to do and do it. As one of my clients, Deborah Dolman once said, "There will always be people to crush your spirit and tell you you can't. Sometimes you've got to let them know they can't stop you.

Other times you've got to get away from them and stay away. And there will be friends you'll have to let go."

Then, throw out all the "shoulds." Simply promise yourself that you'll give everything you do your best shot—because that will be enough. Refuse to allow the word "failure" to penetrate your thinking—ever. There's no such thing, remember? We're all just learning lessons, some we just learn faster than others. Allowing the word "failure" or "fear of failure" to seep into your consciousness just gives you ulcers or worse, if my holistic-health friends are right when they say that much of cancer is related to stress. If you need a therapist to help on this, go find one. To my mind, every woman entrepreneur deserves her own therapist, not to mention masseuse.

TIME OFF

Try to keep your weekends your own—for fun, relaxation, and rest. The most irritable I have ever been was when I spent a year working around the clock and through the weekends. "Dragon Lady" is a euphemism for what I was. The worst. All work and no play made me worse than dull. It made me mean. And it will make you mean.

You need to take time off. At worst, you need a day a week. God did. On that day, let yourself do at least one activity that you'll really enjoy—movie, play, a hike, a romantic dinner— and do it. *Have fun.* It will invigorate you, remind you why you are working so hard and serve as a reward for the sacrifices of time and emotion you are making for the business.

EXERCISE

As I sit here writing, all our beliefs about exercise are fast becoming obsolete. When I grew up, we were taught that the way to exercise was to hit the streets at least three times a week running or biking or aerobicizing until you were totally covered with sweat, until your heart was pounding hard enough for you to hear it, and until part of you started to think that exercise might just lead to an untimely death.

No more. Now, the gurus tell us that twenty minutes of steady walking several times a week should do it. Thank God they've relieved us of the awfulness of the "no pain, no gain" mantra.

You have no excuse. You need exercise. Your body needs you to exercise. Your mind needs you to exercise. Walk every chance you get. You'll find that, aside from the health benefits of walking, you'll build your entrepreneurial stamina. You'll find that you can work solid days without becoming totally exhausted; your thinking will be more clear; you'll make better business decisions. Plus, you'll feel better about yourself.

FOOD AND DRINK

Entrepreneurs need to watch what we put into our mouths. The way I see it, every time you put the wrong food into it, it costs you energy, self-esteem, and possibly your health. Find a nutritionist to guide you. At a minimum, you need to shift to complex carbohydrates (for sustained energy) and away from fats and sugars. I'll personally never give up chocolate, but I know it just adds to the problems. Too much caffeine or caffeine equivalents make you jumpy, irritable, and frenzied. Don't let it be your crutch. Go for a walk in the morning instead. Or drink ice-cold water with a lime in it.

And forget alcohol. At least while you're on the job. Alcohol makes you lose your edge and you can't afford that. It chips away at your concentration and makes most women feel depressed after awhile. It's like a fake drug—it fakes relaxation—while you think the wine is helping you to let go, all it is really doing is stuffing your concerns a little deeper until they manifest themselves as a physical disease later on.

I've really come to respect the impact of alcohol on entrepreneurial women. It can be deadly. First off, we always get drunk faster because we're tired when we drink. Then we start to rely on it as the way to relax until one day, like coffee, we can't do without it. Be extra careful. So many of my clients have problems with alcohol (which many didn't have before) that I actually drive around with information about Alcoholics Anonymous in my car, because I know I'll need it. If you already know that you are an alcoholic, just keep attending those AA meetings religiously. In a way, you are lucky because support groups will help you on all sorts of levels, not just relative to alcohol.

Which brings me to

EMOTIONAL AND SEXUAL VULNERABILITY

You're tough. You make decisions when they need to be made. You manage in a way that would make even a professor at Harvard very proud. You've borrowed money and paid it back. You're selling. To all the world, you have it all.

But. You're tired of being strong. Of making all the decisions minute after minute after minute. Day after day. Of being the one who motivates everyone else. You are, dear reader, amazingly vulnerable emotionally. No one else may know this, but I see it all the time. Women falling in love with their accountants, their attorneys, their bankers. Now, falling in love is not so bad (not that you have the time). What I see is worse. I see entrepreneurs sliding into abusive relationships, and when that happens the business slips. And these are not women the rest of the world expects to fall into abusive relationships. They are attractive, fit, smart, and they live interesting lives. But, they still land in relationships that suck them dry. The problem is that the signs of abuse are not obvious. If they were, most women entrepreneurs would know not to move forward. All of us know to back away from someone who is physically manifesting anger by breaking things and kicking animals, and we're even pretty good at sniffing out psychological abuse when someone calls us useless or stupid or some variation on the theme.

Here are some signs that mean trouble. I put them into a question form so you can ask them of yourself before you get involved.

Sit down. Brace yourself and remember, for your own sake, that honesty really is the best policy.

Did this person you are starting to think of as mate material:

- ☐ Treat your secretary rudely when he called?
- ☐ Ditto for the receptionist?
- ☐ Neglect to introduce you to his friends when you ran into them?
- ☐ Make fun of a waitress or waiter?
- ☐ Or worse, invite your waitress to join you?
- ☐ Flirt with anyone else when he was with you?
- ☐ Control you by telling you what to order?
- ☐ Tell you how to eat?
- ☐ Refuse to talk about himself?
- ☐ Say he would call and didn't?
- ☐ Show up more than fifteen minutes late without an excuse or apology?
- ☐ Or worse, not show up at all?
- ☐ Interrupt you when you started to talk about yourself?

☐ Or worse, simply ignore what you were saying?

☐ Tell you to do things in the same tone someone would use with a three year old? (I know some readers will say to themselves, How can you tell? Believe me, you'll recognize it when it happens.)

☐ Pinch your stomach, thigh, or arm to see how much fat you have?

☐ Make fun of your accomplishments? Or of your business?

☐ Tell you he has no friends (or only one)?

☐ Tell you he hasn't been on a vacation for years?

☐ Refuse to pay for the check at a meal, or just stall long enough so you felt obligated to pay?

☐ Never quite get around to asking you about your day?

Wisdom is always hindsight. The best thing women who have humbled ourselves can do is to forewarn other entrepreneurs of the road traps as we understand them. Falling in love when you are trying to build a business is always untimely. So if you must, at least try to choose someone who isn't abusive, already mated, or too young.

ETHICS

One of the best ways to take care of yourself is always to be true to your values—to hold onto your integrity and honesty through thick and thin—in good times and in not so good times.

Being ethical means choosing to live your life with honesty and integrity. Your intuition will always tell you what to do when you are unclear. Don't think that because you may be new to the business arena that you don't know what the right thing is—you do. Letting someone, anyone, persuade you otherwise is simply selling yourself—and them—short. The following series of questions should help you in situations that are un-clear. I use them to help me understand the real issues of a situation and to sort out the players and then interests:

AN ETHICS TEST

☐ Have you defined the problem accurately? How do you know?

☐ How would you define the problem if you stood on the other side of the fence? How do you know they would define it that way?

☐ How did this situation occur in the first place? From your side? From the other side?

☐ To whom and to what do you give your loyalty?

☐ What is your real intention in making this decision?

☐ How does this intention compare with the probable results?

☐ Whom could your decision or action injure? How can they be injured?

☐ Can you discuss the problem with the affected parties before you make your decision? If you can't, how do you think they'll feel about your decision?

☐ Are you confident that your position will be as valid over a long period as it is now?

☐ Could you disclose, without qualm, your decision or action to your family, friends and society as a whole?

☐ What is the symbolic potential of your action if all the interested parties understood it? What if they misunderstood it?

☐ Under what conditions would you allow exceptions to your stand?

Once you've thought through an issue, if you are still unsure of yourself, find someone you respect and trust and try out your answers on her. A therapist, minister, or other CEO are usually the most helpful counselors here because they have no self-interest in your decision.

ALWAYS LISTEN

The signs of crisis are always there if we just watch. And listen. When you listen, you will discover all the signals before the storm hits. Listen not just for words; you need to listen to your thoughts, to your body, and to the sounds around you. The tones. The silences. The meaning. One of the mistakes we have made in our educational institutions is not teaching our children to listen.

- Listening is hearing the words being said.
- Listening is the ability to say them back in such a way that the speaker says, "Yes, that's what I said."
- Listening is understanding the meanings of the words.
- Listening is understanding the context.
- Listening *is paying attention* to the nonverbal communication that comes with the word; so you can see how important the words are to the speaker.
- Listening is respecting the words, even though you may not like them or want to hear them.

It is so easy to nod and smile and pretend that we're listening to people when in truth we are only half hearing their words. Not listening means you'll need to hear those words over and over until they infiltrate your mind. Not listening means you frustrate everyone around you (because *we know* when someone isn't listening to us), and then the bad attitudes start. Your employees think you don't care (you do—you just weren't listening). Your mate feels the same way. Your banker thinks you're trying to hide something, and your suppliers start to distrust your words. Which leads to headaches and stomachaches and unhappy times for you. The moral here is that it is clearly in your self-interest to listen to your world. Use whatever tricks and reminders you have to. Sometimes I literally sit on my hands so I can't do anything with them to distract my mind when someone is talking to me. One of my clients has a sign that says LISTEN on her desk. You need an equivalent.

CRISIS ADDICTION

Here is my last point regarding taking care of yourself. There is nothing headier than solving a crisis. (Okay, maybe sex is headier, but that's the only thing I can think of.) Suddenly, there's an awfulness surrounding you. Your first reaction is panic—until something inside you tells you to relax and figure out a solution. It's a struggle, but you do. You gather the resources you need. Find the people who can help. Get the poster "Just Do It" out and follow its advice. Then you act on it and *voilà*, the crisis is gone. And you feel terrific. As if you've just climbed a mountain or run a minute mile. Until the next crisis, when it starts all over again. And you solve that. Before you know it, you are addicted to the melodrama—to the situations that test you—and you look forward to them.

Here's what happens to your body. It's similar to always jump-starting your car—it will work, but the cost is frayed nerve endings and your ability to relax. When you can't relax, you lose your balance. The creative you dissipates, and while you may be on a perpetual manic high, you aren't happy. Learn to nip those crises in the bud—by planning, by keeping enough money in the bank, by surrounding yourself with the best people you can afford, and by trusting your intuition. The result will be survival at all levels.

CHAPTER 13

WHERE TO GET

HELP

Whenever I need help I just close my office door, scream every obscenity I know at the top of my lungs, order in chocolate, call my best friend, cry if I can and then make a list of all the people who can help me get out of this ____.
A woman business owner in a calm moment, March 1992

Every book for entrepreneurs I've ever read has ended with a list of resources, so why should I be any different? Remember, you aren't an island. Take help wherever and whenever you find it, remembering to screen for quality and trustworthiness.

YOUR ACCOUNTANT

Always start with your accountant. Every time I see a survey that asks where business owners get their best advice, accountants come out on top. By a lot. The number of owners who turn to their accountants first and foremost ranges from 69 percent to 89 percent, depending on who did the survey. That's why it's so important to have one who understands your business, your industry, and you. If you aren't working with that type of person right now, find another accountant. Make certain that she has helped you to understand your financial reports and that you have a reasonable bookkeeping system. Pay her to show up on your doorstep at least quarterly to see how things are going and to look over your shoulder generally. She'll spot areas where you might be getting sloppy or where you've simply forgotten to pay some costs (like special taxes) or where you're making too much money and it's time to do some investing. Don't hesitate to have her refer you to specialized accountants, as you may need them. An example would be when you decide to start exporting your product.

YOUR ATTORNEY

The same truths hold. Attorneys are right behind accountants in all the surveys about where business owners turn for help. I usually hold off going to my attorney until I think I have a problem with some legal ramifications. In situations where I smell a legal problem emerging, however, I'm on the phone in the next breath. Never hesitate when you think you need to talk to your attorney. When you think you do, you do.

MENTORS

Every business owner deserves a mentor. Mentors are people you've met who have been through what you are going through and have survived to talk about it. Mentors are business owners who have sales, employees, and the respect of both the community and the media. Contrary to what everyone else preaches, I don't believe that you need a formal relationship with a mentor. Instead, I always have the names of several business owners in the community for whom I have a great deal of respect. When I'm in a corner and need help, I just call their office (no, I don't know them personally—and they don't know me), explain to their secretary or assistant what my situation is, and simply ask for a return phone call. *They always call.* That is part of the pure pleasure of a capitalist economy (such as it is) like ours. Business owners actually enjoy helping other business owners—especially one in an underdog position who is trying to work her way out of some mess she's created. Try it. You'll be amazed and, I think, pleasantly surprised by the response you get to a cry for help. Just be very specific about what you are after and *explain it all* to his or her assistant so that person becomes part of your support system too. And don't worry too much about saying thank you. You'll get your turn to help someone else soon enough.

WOMEN'S BUSINESS ASSOCIATIONS

Women know how to help other women. And we want to. On many occasions I have a terrible time trying to finish a training seminar for women business owners because they all get so involved in trying to help each other. It is a wonderful sight to behold. And even better an experience.

There are a wide variety of business groups from which to choose. Try to find a national and a local group where you can participate and take the time to get to know the other women in the group. They will be the group that really understands what you are trying to do with your life when no one else does.

Following is a sampling of organizations you might consider contacting:

- National Association of Women Business Owners, 600 S. Federal St., Suite 400, Chicago, IL 60605, 312-922-0465.

- National Association for Female Executives, 127 W. 24th St., New York, NY 10011, 212-645-0770.

- American Business Women's Association (ABWA), National Headquarters, 9100 Ward Parkway, P.O. Box 8728, Kansas City, MO 64114-0728, 816-361-6621.
- Association of Black Women Entrepreneurs, c/o Corita Communications, P.O. Box 49368, Los Angeles, CA 90049, 213-559-2375.
- Coalition of Women in National and International Business, 1900 L St., N.W., Washington, DC 20036.
- Business and Professional Women's Foundation, 2012 Massachusetts Ave., N.W., Washington, DC 20036.
- Federation of Organizations for Professional Women, 2001 S St., N.W., Suite 540, Washington, DC 20009, 202-328-1415.
- National Association of Black Women Entrepreneurs, c/o Mary French Hubbard, P.O. Box 1375, Detroit, MI 48231, 313-341-7400.
- National Council of Career Women, 3222 N St., N.W., Washington, DC 20007, 202-333-8578.
- National Federation of Business & Professional Women's Clubs, 2012 Massachusetts Ave., N.W., Washington, DC 20036, 202-293-1100.
- The *Inc.* Network. Two-way participation. Call 800-238-1756 to respond to a question posed in a current issue or present a "new query" to the *Inc.* readership.

Closely behind the associations are services aimed directly at women business owners:

- *Nation's Business* Direct Line. This two-page Q&A section in the magazine invites readers to FAX any business-related question. The FAX number is 202-463-3102 or you can mail it to Direct Line, *Nation's Business*, 1615 H St., N.W., Washington, DC 20062.

- Small Business Administrators, Office of Women's Business Ownership, 1441 L Street, N.W., Suite 414, Washington, DC 20416, 202-653-8000. Talk about support for women entrepreneurs! This place is the best—they believe in us and are our advocate in Washington. They deserve flowers every day! The office provides a huge amount of information and help to women, ranging from book lists and pamphlets to training, counseling, and mentors. Get on their mailing list.
- Women's World Banking, 8 W. 40th St., 10th Fl., New York, NY 10018, 212-768-8513.
- The Women's Bureau, U.S. Dept. of Labor, 200 Constitution Ave., N.W., Washington, DC 20210, 202-523-8913.

CHAMBERS OF COMMERCE AND MORE

If you can't find women-oriented programs in your area, and even if you can, it is worth investigating membership in your local Chamber of Commerce. Most chambers offer all sorts of benefits to members, ranging from training programs to counseling to group rates on business and health insurance. Explore yours. I've also found that more and more chambers have women's organizations within the chamber that you can join.

Association organizations related to your industry are worth pursuing as well. They can provide market data, legislative information, and training aimed at your product success. For names of associations, check out the *Encyclopedia of Associations*, which is published by the Gale Research Company in Detroit.

The Small Business Administration has more information than you can probably read in your lifetime. For a catalog, call 1-800-368-5855 or 202-653-7561. The 368-5855 is actually an answer desk where professional advisors are prepared to talk to you about problems you may be having with your business.

- The Young Entrepreneurs Organization, Washington, DC, 202-544-7100, is a membership group for owners of small businesses.

- The National Association of Small Business Investment Companies, Washington, DC, 202-833-8230 is a trade group of investors in small businesses.

- The Association of Small Business Development Centers, 1050 Seventeenth St., N.W., Suite 810, Washington, DC 20036, 202-887-5599—more training and consulting.

- International Franchise Association, World Headquarters, 1350 New York Ave., N.W., Suite 900, Washington, DC 20005, 800-543-1038 for all sorts of information about franchising.

- National Federation of Independent Businesses, 600 Maryland Ave., S.W., Suite 700, Washington, DC 20024, 202-554-9000—your lobbying friends. Since Perot didn't win the election, you'll probably need to get to know these folks and to support them financially.

Finally, don't leave out the local community college. They'll have classes taught by locally successful entrepreneurs and service professionals who have all sorts of knowledge and resources at their fingertips. Plus, you'll meet other entrepreneurs in the class who may be able to help you in some way.

GENERAL SUPPORT GROUPS

As you move along this path of entrepreneurship, you may discover that you want more than business support. Emotional support may be called for as well, particularly if you find your mate distancing, your children forgetting your name, and your facing Thanksgiving alone because you haven't had time to keep up with family and friends. The two types of support groups that seem to work best for women business owners are twelve-step co-dependency groups for spouses of alcoholics or twelve-step programs for women who love too much. I don't know why. I just know, through my own clients, that they are very helpful when you find yourself slamming into some emotional wall you just can't seem to get past.

Which brings me to:

THERAPISTS

Every self-respecting business owner deserves to have a therapist on call. The healthiest women use them, at a minimum, for a sanity check-in once a year or so. Find one. Make sure she is willing to see you at short notice if necessary. (Entrepreneurs can never give anyone a lot of warning for anything.) And don't be afraid to use her. Everytime she helps you to make a decision efficiently and effectively, she is making you money.

PEOPLE YOU TRUST

If I had a magic wand, I would wish for each of you that you be surrounded by people you can trust. Since I don't have a magic wand (yet!), I can only say this: There *are* sharks out there and they do prey on entrepreneurs. They'll offer to write you a business plan you'll never use or raise money for a hefty proportion of what they raise. Or they'll tell you they'll sell your products for you and all you need to do, pretty lady, is sit back and pay them commissions based on their sales—sales that never materialize. Some of these folks will be well-intentioned, but incompetent. Or too tired to muscle through company growth. Some are just slime balls. You need to keep your antennae out all the time. If you aren't sure about someone, it's okay to test them—let them do something small for you to see what happens. Don't depend on anyone until they've earned that. Here's how I measure trust. *Trustworthy people do what they say they will do when they say they will do it.* And they'll give whatever it is their best shot. And when an instance arises where they might not be able to perform as expected, *they'll forewarn you* so you can shift gears or direction.

Get rid of the people around you who can't be trusted. I'd do it for you, but I'm just too far away.

And then watch for the people you can trust. It may be the waitress who told you that you have poppy seeds stuck in your teeth so you don't embarrass yourself going back to work. It may be the friend who warned you about your last relationship as you steamrolled into it. It might be a minister. My most trustworthy adviser is a Korean Zen Buddhist monk who has an uncanny ability to see through any situation I'm in to see the truth—which he then speaks. Go find your monk equivalent. And get rid of the butt-kissers, the groupies, the passive-aggressive types, and the dull. You deserve better.

ON-LINE DATABASE SERVICES

- **BRS**. The business section includes 18 major databases. New users have a menu option. Cost: $80 annually, plus charges ranging from $45 per hour for Disclosure Online to $100 per hour for ABI/Inform. 800-955-0906.

- **CompuServe**. This service offers 350 forums, market quotes, travel information, news, and E-mail. Cost: $8.95 monthly, plus connect charges and additional fees for some services. 800-848-8199.

- **Dialog**. Its nearly 450 databases include TRW Business Credit Profiles, Moody's Corporate Profiles, Disclosure Online, and D&B Donnelly. Cost: $45 start-up fee, plus $35 annually; average individual database rates range from $1.40 to $1.60 per minute. Dialog also sells CD-ROM versions of about 40 databases. 800-334-2564.

- **Dow Jones News/Retrieval.** This service includes *The Wall Street Journal, Barron's,* the *Washington Post,* and Dow Jones News Service. Cost: $29.95 start-up fee, $18 annually after the first year for basic service. In addition, there are per-minute and info-unit charges. With a 2,400-baud modem, charges range from 21 cents to $2.16 per minute, plus 24 cents to 90 cents per 1,000 characters. 609-452-1511.

- **Economic Bulletin Board.** The EBB lists export opportunities and employment, census, and industry statistics. Cost: $35 annually for 300, 1,200, or 2,400 baud, $100 annually for 9,600 baud, plus connect charges. U.S. Department of Commerce, 202-377-1986.

- **GEnie.** Service includes E-mail, an airline-reservation service, and closing stock quotes. Cost: several pricing plans available; fees vary for such services as stock quotes, Charles Schwab Brokerage Services, Official Airline Guides, and Dow Jones News/Retrieval. 800-638-9636.

- **Nexis.** This service offers more than 1,000 sources, including Standard & Poor's, Disclosure Online, Investext, and Predicasts. Cost: $50 monthly, plus additional costs for on-line time.

- **NewsNet.** The service provides some 600 newsletters and 20 news services as well as an electronic clipping service. Cost: $120 annually or $15 monthly plus $1-per-minute connect charge at 300 or 1,200 baud, $1.50 at 2,400 baud, and $2.50 for 9,600 baud. Surcharges for display of copyrighted text range from $.40 to $10 per minute. 800-952-0122.

- **Prodigy.** This easy-to-learn service emphasizes investments and business news. Cost: several pricing plans available; $14.95 monthly for Strategic Investor feature. 800-PRODIGY.

ON COMMITMENT

Until one is committed,
there is hesitancy, the chance to draw back,
always ineffectiveness.

Concerning acts of **initiative** (and creation)
there is one elementary truth
the ignorance of which kills countless ideas
and splendid plans:

That the moment one definitely commits oneself
then Providence moves too.

All sorts of things occur to help one
that would never otherwise have occurred.

A whole stream of events issues from the decision,
raising in one's favor all manner
of unforeseen incidents and meetings
and material assistance
which no man could have dreamt
would come his way.

Whatever you can do, or dream you can, begin it.
Boldness has genius, power, and magic in it.

Begin it now.

—*Goethe*

Commit.

Geraldine Larkin
January 1993

Bibliography

Bennis, Warren, *On Becoming A Leader*. Reading, MA: Addison-Wesley, 1989.

Bliss, Edwin C, *Getting Things Done: The ABC's of Time Management*. New York: Charles Scribner & Sons, 1986.

Collins, James, and William Lazier, *Beyond Entrepreneurship: Turning Your Business into an Enduring Great Company*. Englewood Cliffs, NJ: Prentice Hall, 1992.

Covey, Stephen, *Principle Centered Leadership*. New York: Simon and Schuster, 1992.

DePree, Max, *Leadership is an Art*. New York: Doubleday, 1989.

Dickson, A, *A Woman in Your Own Right*. New York: Quartet Books, 1982.

Godfrey, Joline, *Our Wildest Dreams: Women Entrepreneurs Making Money, Having Fun, Doing Good*. Champaign, Illinois: Harper Business, 1992.

Hanan, Mack, *Fast-Growth Strategies: How to Maximize Profits from Start-Up Through Maturity*. New York: McGraw-Hill, 1987.

Larkin, Geraldine A, *Twelve Simple Steps to a Winning Marketing Plan*. Chicago: Probus Publishing, 1992.

McConkey, Dale D, *No Nonsense Delegation*. New York: Amacom, 1986.

McCormack, Mark H., *What They Don't Teach You at Harvard Business School: Notes from a Street-Smart Executive*. New York: Bantam Books, 1984.

Popcorn, Faith, *The Popcorn Report*. New York: Doubleday, 1991.

Resnik, Paul, *The Small Business Bible*. New York: John Wiley & Sons, 1988.

Sherman, Andrew, *One Step Ahead: The Legal Aspects of Business Growth*. New York: Amacom Books, 1989.

Snyder, E. Kenneth, *Employee Matters: A Legal Guide to Hiring, Firing and Setting Employee Policies*. Chicago: Probus Publishing, 1991.

Spraguis, Ellyn, "How to Fire," *Inc.*, May 1992.

Ury, William, *Getting Past No: Negotiating with Difficult People*. New York: Bantam Books, 1991.

INDEX